MW00776814

To Connie,

Don't underestimate your power
to make change and be
successful. always believe in
yourself.

Breathin'

4/09

Other:

Others an Asian & Pacific Islander Prisoners' Anthology
1st Edition

Printed in Hayward, CA: *Alonzo Printing*
Design and Layout: *Joy Gloria Liu, RevoluXinDesigns.com*
Direction and Editing: *Eddy Zheng, with Ben Wang*
Cover and inside title page artwork include drawing by: Hyung-Rae
Photograph of Eddy Zheng (p. vii), courtesy of Sun-Hyung Lee

Other:

an Asian &
Pacific Islander
Prisoners'
Anthology

Preface *by* HELEN ZIA
Compiled *by* EDDY ZHENG and
the Asian Prisoner Support Committee

Contents

◆ Untitled Drawing (One Koi), *K. D. Huynh*   iv

Thank You, *Eddy Zheng*   v

◆ Asian Prisoners Revolution, *Ou Chiew Saeturn*   vi

Intro, *Eddy Zheng*   vii

Preface, *Helen Zia*   ix

Life   1

From Cambodia with Peace, *Ryan Hem*   3

Adopted American, *Xuliyah Potong*   9

◆ Untitled Drawing (Flame), *K. D. Huynh*   16

Sometimes I Wonder, *Đat Nguyen*   17

Untitled, *Be Trung*   18

Deported Veteran, *Ramonchito T. Velasquez*   22

A Day in the Life, *Viêt Mike Ngo*   25

Autobiography @ 33, *Eddy Zheng*   37

Prison   43

◆ Untitled Drawing (Prison Mask), *Hyung-Rae*   44

A Dose of Raw Reality, *Dámonoa "L.A." Kukisi*   45

I Want People to Know, *Hemnauth Mohabir*   51

◆ Untitled Drawing (Drowning), *Hyung-Rae*   53

Human Rights, *Anonymous South Asian Detainee*   54

Hunger Strike, *Anonymous South Asian Detainee*   55

Torture, *Anonymous South Asian Detainee*   57

Living in a Cage, *Anonymous Female Detainee*   58

Amelioration of Dilapidation, *P. I. R.*   60

✦ Untitled Drawing (Unforgettable), *Hyung-Rae*   62

Unforgettable Experience, *Đat Nguyen*   63

✦ Untitled Drawing (Slave Mentality), *Hyung-Rae*   68

The Slave Mentality, *Dámonoa "L.A." Kukisi*   69

Lesson Learned in Prison College, *Viêt Mike Ngo*   73

Love & Fam   **77**

Can You Understand?, *Xuliyah Potong*   79

Gifts of Love, *Marc Ching*   83

When Will I See Her Again?, *Eddy Zheng*   86

✦ Untitled Drawing (Mother and Child), *Hyung-Rae*   87

Difficult Chanting Sutras, *Eddy Zheng*   89

✦ Untitled Drawing (Tears), *Hyung-Rae*   93

Only in Dreams, *Ricky Thor (Luav Thoj)*   94

✦ Untitled Drawing (Love Forgotten), *Ricky Thor*   96

Waiting, *K.D. Huynh*   97

Have I Ever Told You?, *Teng Ntsis Vang*   98

✦ Untitled Drawing (Flower), *K.D. Huynh*   99

Not Even a Thought, *Teng Ntsis Vang*   100

Npau Suav Txog Koj, *Teeb Ntsis Vaj*   101

Girl, Can I Speak for a Minute?, *Fernando Sumagit*   102

Mom's Unconditional Love, *Fernando Sumagit*   104

Perspectives   **107**

Untitled, *Đat Nguyen*   109

◆ Untitled Drawing (Hope), *Đat Nguyen*   111

To Whom it May Concern, *Đat Nguyen*   112

◆ Untitled Drawing (Mask), *Hyung-Rae*   114

Ghost, *Eddy Zheng*   115

The Real Me, *Viêt Mike Ngo*   116

Red, White and Blue, *Viêt Mike Ngo*   118

Grave Digger, *Viêt Mike Ngo*   119

◆ Untitled Drawing (Hmong), *Ricky Thor*   120

All Around Me, *Ricky Thor*   121

A Place Called Poetry, *Marc Ching*   122

Cut No Corners or Half Step, *Fernando Sumagit*   125

Interview with "Peaches", *Eddy Zheng with Peaches*   127

◆ Untitled Drawing (Two Koi), *K.D. Huynh*   128

Interview with Ou Chiew Saeturn, *Eddy Zheng with Ou Chiew Saeturn*   133

Letter to Ou   134

Outro   **143**

Co-Editor's Note, *Ben Wang*   144

◆ Asian Prisoners Revolution 2, *Ou Chiew Saeturn*   145

More Resources   146

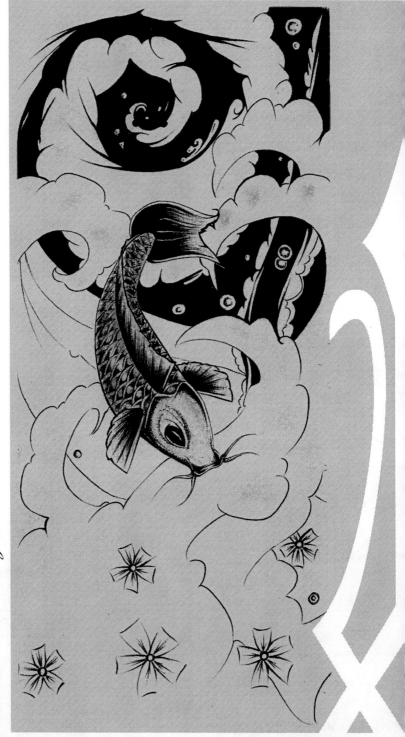

Untitled ◆ *K. D. Huynh* (2005), pen on paper

✦✦✦ Thank You
Eddy Zheng

This anthology would not have been possible without the help of Ben Wang in the free world. Ben took on the responsibilities and challenges of collecting, typing, and editing the writings; applying for a grant; visiting and corresponding with prisoners; gathering support from the Asian community; and keeping me updated with all the progress of the manuscript. Ben's dedication in supporting Asian American prisoners has inspired hope and changes in our lives. Thank you to Helen Zia for her kind support and involvement in this project. Thank you to Joy Liu for offering her talents towards the artistic design and layout of the anthology.

Many thanks to the Asian Prisoner Support Committee members, including Yuri Kochiyama, Wayie Ly, Sun-Hyung Lee, Mike Cheng, Joy Liu, Serena Huang, Rico Remeidio, and others for their support and contributions to the anthology.

Thank you to the Agape Foundation staff, Board of Directors, and volunteers for their generous monetary support of this project.

Special thank you to Professor Darrell Hamamoto of UC Davis, and Professor Harvey Dong of UC Berkeley, for their guidance and support.

As always, I am grateful for the unconditional love and support from my family, guardian Angel Anmol Chaddha, and all of my supporters who continue to sustain me over the years.

As for the contributors of this anthology, thank you for your courage to risk changing yourselves in spite of your incarceration. Please continue to create from your hearts and let your voices be heard. You are not alone.

Last, but not least, thank you, the readers, for allowing us to share our thoughts and stories with you. ✦✦✦

Asian Prisoners Revolution ✦

Ou Chiew Saeturn, pencil on paper

✦ ✦ ✦ Intro

Eddy Zheng

Revolution is violent.

Revolution is painful.

Revolution is a constant and courageous process of transformation within oneself.

Whenever people are living under a system of oppression, everyone has the inalienable right to overthrow it by any means necessary.

We must engage in a personal revolution before we can march towards a collective revolution.

For the past 20 years, I've witnessed the steady rise of the Asian American population in the prison system, especially Southeast Asians. This is a problem that has often been neglected by the mainstream media and the Asian communities. Due to cultural differences and traditions, Asian prisoners have become lepers of their own communities. We're left to survive by ourselves with minimum support from our families. Most guys in here don't know how to reach out and those few who do find little response. I have come to the conclusion that the lack of interest from the Asian American community is its need to stay in the glass house of blissful ignorance. It's easier to neglect the problem that causes shame to its model minority status than address

it. The result is the multiplying of "Asian Leprosy" in this modern day slave plantation of the Prison Industrial Complex and the continued victimization of the Asian community.

That's why I wanted to publish an anthology of Asian American prisoners' writings. I wanted to give the lepers an opportunity to show the Asian community that beneath the plague of leprosy they're good people. With help, they can change and become productive members of society.

This anthology of essays, vignettes, poems, interviews, and drawings you are about to read is the fruition of individual revolutions that Asian American prisoners have undertaken. All of the contributors, during their time of incarceration, have consciously decided to topple the system of oppression that has caged them mentally. They have gone through a revolution within themselves by taking a fearless inventory of their lives and deconstructing the origin of their oppression. As a result, they have been able to bare their souls to the world through their creativities. ✦ ✦ ✦

All proceeds generated from the sale of this book will be donated towards disaster relief aid and prisoner support work.

Preface

Helen Zia

When I first met Eddy Zheng, one of the contributors to this anthology, he was 35 years old, clean-cut and sociable, dressed in a neat blue denim shirt and jeans. In another life, he might have been an eager young professional, a smart and hopeful Asian American on the rise. At that moment, however, he was greeting me from the other side of the security gate in the visiting area of the California state prison where he was incarcerated.

Eddy was already 18 years into a seven-to-life sentence which he received when he was a juvenile offender tried as an adult for committing a home invasion-style robbery and kidnapping. Now a middle-aged adult, Eddy has had many years to reflect upon his crime and his life. He learned English, took every self-help class available in prison, earning a GED and college degree. He and the other poets, writers and artists in this collection found their voices through creative expression. Their messages are poignant, critical and important for all to hear.

Yet in mainstream news media and ethnic media alike, stories about people like Eddy cannot be found. In their media-filtered world, it is as though incarcerated Asian Americans do not exist, and the public is all too willing to accept their invisibility. Even within the criminal justice system, Asian American prisoners are treated as though they are invisible. They are not counted in most statistics from the local to federal levels, and, consequently, they do not count. They are categorized as "Other" in a governmental system that recognizes only "black, white, Hispanic and Other."

Failing to count imprisoned Asian Americans and Pacific Islanders keeps them hidden from view—even from their own communities. Lumping them together as "Other" ensures that any cultural or linguistic needs they have will be ignored. Casting them as alien "Others" maintains a perpetual alien status and keeps them from ever being seen as full persons. As Asian Americans, they are rendered doubly invisible—and Pacific Islanders even more—by the prevailing stereotype of the "model minority." This false but persistent image reduces all Asian Americans and Pacific Islanders to the super successful achieving "good" minority who never has problems, challenges or ends up behind bars.

By all such accounts that permeate the conventional wisdom, countless incarcerated Asian Americans and Pacific Islanders should not exist.

But they do—and they reflect the full range of humanity of the Asian American and Pacific Islander communities. The contributors to this anthology are Cambodian, Chinese, Filipino, Hmong, Japanese, Korean, Laotian, Mien*, Tongan, Vietnamese; some are immigrant, refugees, indigenous or adopted. One is transgender, another is female; Asian American and Pacific Islander women and girls are also part of the prison population.

Many of the contributors, like Eddy, were latch-key children of laboring or absentee parents, forced to develop their own survival skills in tough neighborhoods. Some entered the juvenile justice system speaking little English, with parents who spoke even less English and possessed no understanding of the legal system. Many Asian American and Pacific Islander parents don't know that they are entitled to interpreters and public defenders. Some believe they should do whatever police and prosecutors say, such as agreeing to let their juvenile children be tried as adults and plead guilty to all charges.

In San Francisco, a consortium of non-profit youth centers and advocates called Services and Advocacy for Asian Youth (SAAY) reported in 2004 that while arrests of African American, Native American and Caucasian youth have decreased nationally, arrests of Asian and Pacific Islander boys and girls have increased by 11.4%. Yet many youth advocates and juvenile justice professionals say that the Asian American community is in denial about the problems that Asian American and Pacific Islander youth face.

Sometimes families won't acknowledge problems at home because of shame and social stigma; meanwhile the broader society ignores issues that don't fit the image of the model minority Asian Americans. Professionals like Patricia Lee, a San Francisco public defender, expect the situation to get worse if nothing is done, in part because Asian American youth are fighting back more often when they are picked on. SAAY statistics show that although Asian American arrest rates overall are lower than other racial groups, their conviction rates are 28% higher and they are placed into institutions at significantly higher rates than African American, Hispanic or white youth.

In spite of community stigma, media ignorance, and deceptive stereotypes that conspire to silence incarcerated Asian American and Pacific Islanders, these inmates are making themselves heard in this important collection. Their poetry and prose, drawings and letters all inform with their stories, hopes and fears; they teach us through the sharp insights they've gained from doing time in a part of American society that few Asian Americans acknowledge, and where few Americans recognize Asian Americans and Pacific Islanders.

These compelling voices, now unleashed, make for a more complete picture of Asian Americans and Pacific Islanders. Listen closely to what they have to say-you will be moved, perhaps to action. These members of our communities must no longer be relegated to "Other," for they are part of us all.

✦ ✦ ✦

* Although there has been some concern over the use of the term "Mien" due to negative connotations derived from its historical roots, we do include it in this anthology since it is the term used by Ou Chiew Saeturn, the sole Mien contributor to this book.

Helen Zia is the author of Asian American Dreams: The Emergence of an American People (Farrar Straus Giroux, 2000). She has also written about the politically-motivated prosecution and incarceration of Dr. Wen Ho Lee, the Chinese American nuclear scientist who was falsely accused of being a spy for China; with him she coauthored My Country Versus Me (Hyperion, 2002).

Life

From Cambodia with Peace

Ryan Hem

When I was first incarcerated, my father disowned me. I lost all my friends. I felt like an animal that was locked up waiting to be slaughtered. For over five years, I was told when to eat, when to get up, and when to sleep. I hit bottom. I thought of doing a lot of things to myself including suicide. Everyone around me had problems. I heard all kinds of stories, many which I didn't want to hear. The hardest thing for me was not knowing when I would have my freedom again. This is my story.

I was born right into the beginning of a civil war in Cambodia. When the Khmer Rouge took over, I was taken away from my family to live among other children. The Khmer Rouge put us to work and taught us the way to kill our parents. They said that our parents hate us and that was why we were taken away from them. The Khmer Rouge said they were there to protect us. Even though I was little, I remembered most of what was going on. I saw the Khmer Rouge torture and kill people. There was one frightening torture I witnessed which I can never forget. As I was walking back to our campground, I came across a young man that was hung upside-down from a tree branch. His hands were tied behind his back and he was screaming for his life. Four young Khmer Rouge soldiers stood around him laughing, as one soldier slit the man's throat with a machete.

At the end of 1978, Vietnamese soldiers came through our town with lots of big guns. There were many of them around and the Khmer Rouge were somehow missing. That was when I met my parents. I did not remember them that well, but they knew who I was. Running around naked herding cattle and water buffalos in the green fields of Phnom Somphov was how I remembered my childhood with my parents.

After spending time in Thailand and the Philippines, my family arrived in the good old USA. My family eventually settled in Stockton, CA. Growing up as a teen in the States was especially hard living in a neighborhood of drug dealers and alcoholics. They always beat me up on my way to school. They would steal my bike and throw my books away. Soon enough, I was asked to join the Asian gang to be protected. I did not join the gang but I do have friends that did. School went sour for me by 11th grade. I stopped wanting to go to school. My parents did not want to move, so I went on my own.

I was working and traveling. I did not know what I was looking for. I felt I needed to keep on going. I went to Massachusetts, Dallas, Seattle, Anchorage, Honolulu, and back to Texas. I got caught up with some friends who were making big money. They were buying and selling stolen computer chips. I went to work with them and made a lot of money. I bought a nice BMW, traveled between California and Texas for this illegal activity, and got drunk every night. I knew I was going to get caught someday. But I couldn't stop even if I wanted to. I would be dead if I had stopped. Soon enough most of the guys that I was dealing with got caught. They told the FBI and I was busted.

It took one or two months before my parents found out that I was picked up. When my dad found out, he was so angry he couldn't talk to me. When he did speak to me on the phone, he said in Khmer (he always spoke in Khmer when he had something serious to say), "You are no longer my son! You disgraced me and you disgraced my family. I'd never thought you, my son would do something to disgrace the family's name." I cried when he said that. It hurt, but he had the right to say it because I had let him down.

> **When he did speak to me... he said in Khmer (he always spoke in Khmer when he had something serious to say), *"You are no longer my son."***

Every time I thought about my family, I would cry. I'd have feelings of regret and sorrow – not just for myself but for my family. All these things came back to me and when it hit, the tears just flowed. I hit the bottom of my life. When my dad disowned me I felt I should have been killed in the war so that he and my mom wouldn't have to put up with me. I would take death over hearing my father say that he would disown me. I tell you, knowing I had no family made me unafraid of anyone throughout my incarcerated time.

It was during my third year in prison that I was asked to attend a Buddhist service and I started doing meditation. We just sat in a circle. No one said anything and I didn't know what was going on. I was confused at first, but I liked it. We just sat and no one said a word, not even the monk.

I didn't know what it was, but I liked the quietness and the peacefulness. We would sit there a whole hour in meditation group and I didn't feel the time pass. I started doing it in my cell sometimes even in lockdown or sleep time. I wouldn't sleep. I would just sit and try to get that feeling of emptiness, of peacefulness - when all you hear is the sound of your breathing. After you come out of it, you feel different. It's like you've had an injection of energy. You don't look at things and judge them anymore. If you look at an object like a book, well, it is just a book. What is, is. I looked at my whole life and I saw it as just a life. I don't judge my life anymore and feel badly or feel good about things. Bad or good, I look at the moments and I don't judge it. Its just life. I just go with the flow. That gave me the strength to get through day by day. I grabbed reality in the moment. When you do that - when you live life in the moment, it makes time fly fast.

I realized that meditation gave me power that I didn't have before. It gave me will power to control my actions, including thinking and being aware of my surroundings. This is precious to me. I gave up smoking cold turkey. That was something I couldn't do before. I could be happy being incarcerated or I could be an ass and just give everyone a hard time. Meditation is just like taking the trash out. If you can go about your daily routines with a clear mind, you're happy.

I am not a religious person, but learning the meditation was my strength. I was hooked on meditation ever since. It is what it is! Let it be and you're in peace. I said whenever I get out of incarceration, I will be the happiest person on earth. Guest what, I'm very happy now.

I did most of my sentenced time and was then taken to INS and deported back to Cambodia. I was one of 12 Cambodians in the second group to be deported back to Cambodia. When the deportation came, I had already picked up what I needed to know to meditate on my own. In a way, I was looking forward to the change, but I didn't expect much. I was going with the flow. At INS, a lot of the other guys were afraid of being deported, but I was enjoying the change of being in the new facility, going into the yard, the good food, and music. I stopped myself from letting my feelings make me want too much.

Once I got out of detention here in Cambodia, I called my mom and dad, and my dad spoke to me for the first time since I went to prison in 1997. I think my mom got my dad to speak to me. His voice sounded normal when he spoke to me, but with a caring personality. We just talked a little about his contacts and connections here and I asked him about his health. He was still keeping his feelings hidden. Neither of us had to say we were sorry. We were just father and son. Then I hung up the phone and I felt happy. I went home and I just sat with that feeling. It was the greatest feeling.

And then I started talking more and more to both my parents and eventually they put me on the speaker phone when I called. I would say, "I love you everybody. Dad, I love you." He never said anything back, but I thought I would just keep throwing that out there. Finally, one day he responded. He actually picked up the phone and said, "I love you too, and take good care of yourself."

After getting out of detention, I stayed in Phnom Penh for a few weeks, and then I relocated to Siem Reap (the second biggest city in Cambodia). There I met my girlfriend Mov. She was my favorite tour guide out of the 6 girls that I was with that day. We clicked and went everywhere together. We had so much fun together. I felt very comfortable being with her and I felt she was the best to bring home, so I didn't let time pass me by. I got her to go out with me almost every other day and she became my girlfriend. When I got an apartment I invited her many times to stay with me. Soon enough she agreed and that was after she had spoken with my parents.

Later, when I told my parents that my girlfriend was pregnant, my dad took full charge of most phone calls. Now he is the one who calls me and asks to speak to my daughter.

My life is better now that it has value and a sense of fulfillment. Everything I do I make sure it's a good deed either for me or for someone around me. I've seen very little of my good side, so I am dedicated to seeing more. I have my family, Brenda my daughter, and Mov my wife.

We are poor, but we are happy.

Peace ✦ ✦ ✦

Adopted American

Xuliyah Potong

I often wonder what it would feel like to roam on the soil where my ancestors bled. If the air I breathed in would smell sweeter or if I'd experience a transformation rushing through my entire being. This moment has always only been as elusive as a mirage to me up to this point in my life; a distant illumination that dissipates like misty fog whenever I claw futily to grasp a hold. As I sit in this cage and no longer actively participate in life but merely observe the surreal circumstances that propel me forward, it has become clear that the scenery I've only beheld in my reverie will now take physical shape and await my entrance. Life as I used to know it is over. The carefree days on American streets will now give way to uncertain nights in a foreign country that is to be my new home, Laos.

After seven arduous years of incarceration, I am finally on the cusp of my emancipation. Unfortunately, this freedom that I have been patiently suffering to embrace does not come without a price. Upon completion of my sentence, I will immediately be transferred from State Prison into Federal custody where proceedings concerning my residency status in America will begin. Because of my criminal conviction, I am now facing imminent deportation.

Officially, there are two options available to me: I can

decide on further litigation and fight to stay in America, or I can waive this right and agree to be deported. Practically speaking, I have no choices. The crime I am convicted of is categorized as an "aggravated felony", and if designated as such, is almost iron-clad in precluding one from averting deportation through judicial means. Although I have accepted that my days in America are numbered, I can't help but hang on to the hope that maybe, I will once again be accepted for the flawed person I always was.

Ever since the 18th century, Laos has been subjected to foreign colonial rule. It was first victimized by its larger neighbor to the west, Thailand, which in turn was succeeded by France and then Japan. Not until 1954 was Laos granted autonomy under the Geneva Accords. This newfound independence only brought to light the ensuing scramble for power that would unfold between competing political factions the world over. It was right around this time that the Communist and non-Communist blocs of the Cold War era were beginning to take shape. The United States, as the leader of the non-Communist countries, was particularly concerned with limiting the advances of Communism in Southeast Asia. Despite the contentious political climate swirling all around them, the Communist Pathet Lao, neutralists, and pro-Western Lao government officials still managed to compromise and set up a coalition government. However, due to American paranoia and instigation, this tentative arrangement did not last for long. Opposed to any accommodation of the Communist Pathet Lao, the U.S. actively sponsored and encouraged an anti-Communist group to overthrow the existing government. This blatant disregard for Laos sovereignty compelled the Pathet Lao and neutralists to turn to Russia and its Communist allies

If it is indeed true that it takes a whole village to raise one child, then what village is ultimately responsible for rehabilitating its wayward youth?

for aid in resuming guerrilla warfare. Eventually, after more than twenty years of intermittent civil war, the Pathet Lao finally seized power as America pulled out from the region and all of Southeast Asia fell like dominoes to Communism.

After establishing control, the Pathet Lao did not automatically cease their campaign of bloodshed. They continuously hunted and sought to eliminate any remaining soldiers that had opposed them. My father was one of these soldiers. Left with no other alternative but to escape, he – together with my pregnant mother and eldest sister – led the way through treacherous terrain and land mine-laden jungles. They had to gingerly navigate their way into Thailand, fearfully evading detection by the Pathet Lao and getting cut down by machine-guns. Awaiting them in Thailand were refugee camps set up to accommodate the hundreds of thousands of displaced citizens from Laos, Cambodia, and Vietnam. While residing at these camps, refugees were not permitted to travel freely beyond the confines of their designated area. Integrating into Thai society was prohibited. This was merely a temporary layover, pending permanent resettlement in the U.S. or any other Western country willing to accept them. As chance would have it, I was conceived and given birth to during our stay in the refugee camp. On January 17, 1980, when I was at the age of five months, my family and I arrived in California.

Life in America has not always been easy. Growing up in an ethnic enclave with parents who couldn't speak English presented barriers I failed to fully appreciate until reaching adulthood. In spite of this, I have always been aware of how blessed we were to be living in America. My parents never let me forget the trials they had to endure in order to get us here, just so we would not be exposed to the harsh realities of life in Laos. Because of these admonitions, I knew that simply being in America was a privilege that would afford me the opportunities to overcome whatever obstacles I may encounter. With the education I received in school and the abundant resources available for furthering my education; as an adolescent I believed the possibilities for my life were limitless. I had dreams of succeeding in any number of professions, and even dared to envision that I might one day help find a cure for asthma; a disease that claimed the life of my mother and has ailed me since childhood. These ambitions were driven by my motivation to instill pride in my parents by displaying that all their sacrifices were not made in vain.

I cannot recall exactly when it was that I started to stray from the path that was paved for me. Going against everything I was taught, I engaged in behavior that would have appalled my mother were she to ever discover. I joined a gang and did things that adversely affected the lives of countless people. This downward spiral continued until it landed me where I am today. During the entire time that I was facing a life sentence, the one thing I longed for most was a second chance to make amends for all my former misdeeds. It was during this period that I realized how destructive I had been. I had complete disregard for how precious life is—the lives of those within my community and my own.

The reality of not ever being able to call America my home again is very difficult for me to digest. It feels as though my adoptive parents are banishing me from the home I've spent my entire life in...

This is something shamefully demonstrated by the crime I committed. The punishment I received was more than just. I deserved to serve every last day of my sentence. Throughout this entire tragedy, never was I the victim. The victims are those who have been irrevocably damaged by my actions. If only it were possible to undo all that has transpired...

I love America. Although I was not born here and am not officially a citizen, it is still the only home I've ever known. I am grateful that America adopted me and provided salvation for my family at a time when death lurked ominously behind every turn. The thought of making a life anywhere else has never even entered my mind. It was not until after my arrest that I became aware of my vulnerability to deportation. This myopic ignorance is the main culprit behind why I never took advantage of my many chances to become a citizen. The reality of not ever being able to call America my home again is very difficult for me to digest. It feels as though my adoptive parents are banishing me from the home I've spent my entire life in and sending me away to biological parents who are virtual strangers. All because they cannot forgive me. If it is indeed true that it takes a whole village to raise one child, then what village is ultimately responsible for rehabilitating its wayward youth? This assignment should not be delegated to a third party. I am the product of American society, not Laotian. My expulsion will not only create an irreparable disconnect with America, it will also separate me from my family. How can I be expected to survive in a country where I am illiterate and am all by myself? The authoritarian regime that tried to exterminate my family is still entrenched in power. The very same government that America saved us from is now the one it wants to deliver me to?

I never fathomed that this could be my fate. I have already forfeited my youth because of a tragic mistake that I made. Now I must serve another sentence of being barred from America for life. Like a desperate child who has lost his way, I just want to go home. Instead, it is with profound sadness that I return to my ancestors in disgrace. ✦ ✦ ✦

Addendum

At the time that the writer wrote this piece, he was under the false impression that he would be deported to Laos. Xuliyah was taken immediately into Homeland Security/Immigration & Customs Enforcment's detention facilities (formerly INS) after he completed his prison sentence, but because Laos does not currently have a repatriation agreement with the United States to take back people who are deported, he was NOT deported to Laos. After several months of detention, Xuliyah was released and is now in the process of incorporating back into his community. However, in order to be released from detention, Xuliyah did sign an order of removal. What this means is that if Laos ever signs a repatriation agreement with the U.S., Xuliyah will be put on a list to be deported back to Laos.

Many API prisoners face the same difficult questions that Xuliyah encountered: do they fight their deportation order and remain imprisoned in an INS jail for an indefinite amount of time, with no guarantee of winning their case? Or do they sign their order of removal and face being deported to a country that they barely have any memory of, don't know the language, and have limited family support for? The high cost of lawyer fees to fight a case leave most people with no other choice but to sign their order of removal.

The passage of anti-immigrant legislation in 1996 and the heightened paranoia against non-citizens since September 11, 2001, have set the stage for the increased deportation of our communities. Non-citizen, legal residents who have committed an "aggravated felony" are now mandatorily deportable and have lost the right to an independent judicial review in the immigration courts. An aggravated felony can include any crime that was given a sentence of one year or more (down from five years pre-1996)—even non-violent crimes such as shoplifting and auto theft.

A large number of non-citizen Cambodian Americans who signed their orders of removal, thinking that an agreement would never be signed, were forcibly deported after the U.S.-Cambodia repatriation agreement of March 2002. Many Laotian and Vietnamese Americans with orders of removal fear that they will be next. Laos and Vietnam are the only two Asian countries at this time that do not have a repatriation agreement with the United States.

Untitled ◆ *K. D. Huynh,* color pencil on paper

Sometimes I Wonder

Dạt Nguyen

Sometimes I wonder, the day I die
where will I be, will anyone cry?
Will I be missed
or am I just another memory?
My reality is gated and walled from society.
Over the years I've been doing a lot of growing up
remember the tears from my mother's eyes as they led
me away in cuffs.
My first understanding of a book was behind walls
isolated from the world made my imagination soar.
I read on the outs but I couldn't comprehend
I could write, but it was just the competence of my pen.
Education was not my plan
being hard and down was my vision of a man.
Props and praised for my bad behaviors
little did I know I was on the road to failure.
Now whenever I write my people a letter
I let them know their youngest son is getting better
intellectually, physically, and mentally
and I won't fall victim to misery.
Even though I'm not free physically
I learn to escape it mentally
'cause misery loves company
but I refused to let others shape my destiny.

❖ ❖ ❖

Untitled

Be Trung

My name is Be Trung and I was born in Vietnam in 1977. I arrived in the United States in 1979 at the age of two years. My mother and father thought it was best to start our lives in America where there would be many opportunities for us to live a good life here. In Vietnam, there are not too many opportunities there to make a whole lot of money.

The first city in the United States where we arrived was Kansas City. We stayed there with some other family that was good enough to be our sponsor family in the United States. We lived in Kansas City for about 4 to 5 years to save enough to start off on our own. My mom and dad worked long and hard to save as much money as they can. At the same time, they are taking care of me and my two older sisters. My mom and dad came to the United States with very little and had to do their best to basically make something out of it. As the years go by, my parents saved up enough money to be able to move out on our own. We then moved to Oakland, California where my parents rented a small little apartment where all five of us would have to live in. My parents struggled for many and many years until then they saved enough money to rent a house with my aunt and uncle.

I grew up not really having much. My parents got on welfare to help us get by and be able to save up money at the same time. Me and my older sister did not have any fancy clothes and stuff growing up. We barely had any toys to play with because my parents couldn't afford it. As I reached Junior High, I began to smoke weed and hang around gangs and get in trouble. I got arrested a lot as a juvenile going in and out of juvenile hall all the time. I cut school all the time, stole cars, and just did everything there is that is bad. I had no cares in the world when I was young. I thought as I got older, I would grow out of all this trouble, but everything had just begun. At 17 years old, my parents moved to Union City and they thought that by moving out of the ghetto that my life would get better, but it seems like it got worse.

I started using crystal meth at the age of 20 years old. I have been using the drug for about 7 years now. I even started selling drugs to support my own habit and make only a little money. I did all that mainly to support my own habit. I went in and out of county jail numerous times and finally went to state prison. Although I only spent 3 months in prison, it was enough to show me that it is not a place to be. I know that if I don't stop using drugs that there will be many more trips to prison for me. It is going to be hard, but I have to stop using drugs. I use drugs to make me feel good and to help make me forget about all of my problems. It makes me feel like there is no problem at all. Day after day, I look to get my next high. Once the drug wears off, that is when reality comes at you at 150 mph and hits you straight in the face. I have lots of fun with using drugs, but I am blinded to see that it is ruining my life and making it worse at every hit I take. I have to admit that I am not going to be able to quit this drug on my own. I am going to need some help with this. I don't know exactly how I am going to do it, but it will be done. Drugs have changed me and my life quite a bit. It has made me grumpy, moody, and a little crazy. It has made me change into a whole new person for the worst, not the best. I look at myself all the time when I am on drugs and I tell myself, "Why am I doing this to myself?" It is like my mind knows what is the right thing to do, but my body does not want to react to it.

So far, I have lost a lot from this drug. I have lost trust from my family, friends, and a lot of respect from my loved ones. It eats me up inside every day. I think about what I have become. But that is one thing about me, I don't give up at nothing. I have seen a lot of people that use drugs that have given up trying to quit and just accept the fact that there is no hope. I am not going to be one of those people. I want what everyone wants in life and that is mainly happiness and peace.

After being done with my time in state prison, I found that I have an immigration hold and had to go to INS jail to await my hearing on whether to deport me or stay in the United States. I never expected this to happen. My parents even warned me on how if I don't stop getting in trouble they are going to kick me out of this country. I thought that I had to do a really serious crime for them to even consider deporting me. I guess I was wrong and should have listened to my parents. That is one of the billion things my parents are right about again.

As I am locked up at an INS facility, I talk to other inmates on what I should do or try to see if anyone has a similar case as mine to get some advice on what I should do. From what I found out, they cannot deport me because my country Vietnam does not accept anyone back. Vietnam is communist, so the most they can keep me for is 90 days, then they would have to cut me loose. The bad thing about signing the deportation paper is that you lose your chance of getting citizenship and you lose your green card. Most people in here have everything here in the United States. As for me, I spent most of my life in America. All my family are in America. I have nobody else. That is not fair for America to try to deport someone that has spent most of their life here in America. We are only human and we all make mistakes. It is part of life. Nobody is perfect. As I am going on my fourth month here still waiting for some results, I feel like my time is coming soon, but don't really know exactly when. My 90 day review is coming up real soon, so I hope I get some good news.

Another bad thing about INS is that they hold you so far away from your family. As for me, I am about 3-4 hours away from where I live. My family and daughter don't really have the time to drive so far away; I miss them. I haven't been able to see them for about 6 months now. My family is trying to do all they can right now to do whatever they can to help me stay in America. I call home every once and awhile to check up on how my parents, family, and daughter are doing. Not everyone that is in INS committed a crime to be in here. There are some people that left America for a vacation and when they came back, INS came and arrested them for illegal entry. Even if they have all the documents they need to leave the country for a little while. I feel that America should consider a different way to deal with people that aren't a citizen of the United States. They need to realize that they are not just taking us away from our kids, family, and loved ones, but they are taking our whole life away from us. Everything we have is in America. So as I end this here, all I can do now is just wait and hopefully see some good results soon. ✦ ✦ ✦

Deported Veteran

Ramonchito T. Velasquez

My name is Ramonchito T. Velasquez. I am 44 years old and a U.S. Army veteran. I came to the United States on Dec. 31, 1973 at the age of 13.

I joined the U.S. Army on an "early entry program," one year prior to my highschool graduation. I am the second generation in my family to become a serviceman, following my Grandfather who served during the WWII Japanese occupation in the Philippines. He was part of the Philippine Scouts who helped the Americans defeat the opposing forces of the Japanese empire. This granted him U.S. citizenship, which was to be the greatest achievement my grandfather did for all of us who are presently residing in this "land of opportunity." It was an honor for me to continue the tradition of serving this nation that gave us the chance to change our lives forever from this generation to the next.

I served my active duties from 1979-1984. I did my overseas tour of duty in Germany and the following two years in Washington State. I completed my full service term in 1985, when I acquired my Honorable Discharge certificate. I joined the military for the same reason that my grandfather did - to petition my family, mother, brothers and sisters to come to the U.S.

I loved this country and didn't know any place in this world that I could call my home other than in the U.S. But now, after 33 years of living in this country, the American dream is now becoming a nightmare. One by one, my world is closing in on me. I am confined in a 5 x 10 cell where I am constantly locked in, against my will. I have made a lot of mistakes in my life that I mostly regret. I have become a bi-product of growing up in America - being a gang member, a drug user and a burden to my family.

During the past couple of years (2003-2005), I have admitted to crimes that I was found guilty of (by association) - possession for sale of the controlled substance of methamphetamine. I served my sentence and was put on a supervised probationary period. Unfortunately, I have failed to comply by the rules and violated my probation. I was arrested and sentenced to 16 months in State Prison with time credit served. I later realized that my constitutional rights had been violated for misinforming me of the conditions of my sentence. The court of law failed to inform me that being sentenced to over 365 days (one year) would jeopardize my residential status in this country. I am most likely to be deported back to the Philippines, due to being a non-citizen of the U.S.

I can hardly believe that my main adversary is the U.S. government itself - the same government that I dedicated six years of my life to serving. I am being held by the Department of Homeland Security (DHS)/Immigration & Customs Enforcement (ICE), (formerly INS), after already serving time and paying my dues for the crimes charged against me. DHS/ICE has detained me longer than my prison term. My question is "why am I being held in jail, when all I'm trying to do is stay in this country with my loved ones?"

I thought this country believes in "patriotism". Apparently, in my opinion, that is a misrepresentation for those who do. Broken hearts and shattered dreams is what I am being compensated for my service in the military.

The INS judge says that because of my case of "aggravated felony," there's no chance of any compromising regarding my residency. I was told that I was not eligible for anything that

would help me remain in in the United States.

I feel as if I have been used and abused by the government. I have been demoralized and torn apart from my very existence.

I only wish for one thing before I leave my whole life behind... I wish that my story will be heard and hope that someone, somewhere who has any authority to change this unfairness for those whom have served will be granted some kind of immunity or second chance to re-live that American dream. ✦ ✦ ✦

A Day in the Life

Việt Mike Ngo

"Don't walk away mad, just walk away!" June says, laughing in the passenger seat. Peter slams the driver's side door and storms into the liquor store, not liking Jr.'s comment about him being a beer gopher. Sitting in the back seat, Tuna and I smile at each other, shaking our heads. There's never peace between those two. Tuna's smile leaks into a grimace. I know I look the same even before I follow his eyes to the barrel of a nickel-plated revolver pointing inside the driver's side window—a gang rival caught us slipping. A neon Budweiser sign flickering from a bad connection, reflects off the mirror polish of the barrel, mimicking the rhythm of my heartbeat. This Buds not for me, I pray. I look at the inside of my coffin—a two-door, hatch-back Datsun. The barrel nods. "Remember me?" says Nickel-plate. June explodes out of the passenger side door as a white flash floods the inside of the car.

"BOOM!"

I bolt out of bed, kneeing my metal locker inches above my legs. Cursing my neighbor for slamming his cell door, I lay back down and resign myself to the truth that escape in dreams is as futile as escape in reality. Five gun towers and twenty foot high walls are my daily reminder of the latter. I soak in my surroundings as the last traces of the streets wear off. My cell: two beds, one on top of the other, a sink, a shitter, and two lockers, all inside a space eleven feet long, four and a half feet wide, and eight feet high— from one coffin to another. I crawl off the top bunk and get ready for work in a lifeless, gray twilight.

While brushing my teeth, a nasally, female keen begins its daily, drawn out announcement that North Block inmates have ten minutes to exit their cells and get to work or face the consequences. I gag. If given a wish at that moment, a wish for a muzzle to silence the banshee on the P.A. system would beat out a wish for a parole date. I grab my walkman and a Neruda book and exit the cell as my cellie enters. My cellie greets me with a smile and a good morning. I give a weak grunt and leave. I understand married couples have mornings when their partner's presence is sickening. You can imagine how prisoners forced to live with each other must feel.

> I understand married couples have mornings when their partner's presence is sickening. You can imagine how prisoners forced to live with each other must feel.

Ducking and dodging mental patients who double as prisoners—men who are still affected by last night's psych meds—I make my way out of the musty housing unit. Walking up and out of the sunken dungeon, the slate-gray, overcast sky reminds me of climbing out of the Datsun eleven years ago. That day, anger, frustration, and mostly fear wrapped itself around a cold ball of lead in the pit of my stomach. If Peter hadn't come out of the liquor store shooting, who knows what would've happened. As it was, Nickel-plate retreated behind a car, shot back at Peter and disappeared around some bushes, hitting nothing but the liquor store. On my way home that night, I promised myself two things: Make Nickel-plate regret not killing me and never again get caught in such a helpless position as in the back seat of a parked car with a magnum 357 drawn on me. I should've known that by exacting vengeance on my rival, I would then find myself in yet another helpless position—

indefinitely. But instead of a parked car and a 357, it's now a recreational yard and five sniper rifles.

Three steps outside the housing unit, two guards are checking IDs, laundry bags, prisoners' destinations, anything and everything they want. They are yard cops and my immediate bosses. My job mainly consists of typing write-ups—written infractions against prisoners accused of rule violations. Being one of three of their clerks, my work load is minimal. The majority of the day I spend reading, writing, exercising, things that benefit me, not my captors— the main reason I vied for this job. There is one drawback. In typing a write-up, I'm technically assisting in lengthening a prisoner's captivity, a task I abhor and struggle with daily.

My bosses are in the middle of a joke as I check-in, "You see the look on his face when I told him to get naked?!" This is a tactic used to intimidate prisoners with attitudes. The official reasoning for the unclothed body search is that the prisoner seems suspicious. The truth is the guards didn't like seeing the anger and frustration on the prisoner's face when he was ordered to have his possessions searched.

They smile at me and I return the same. My smile, however, is tempered with the knowledge that the unfortunate prisoner could've been me if I wasn't their clerk. In between laughs, the taller of the two says the Squad has a write-up for me, then hands me a paper bag. The Squad is California Department of Correction's CIA, FBI, and DEA all rolled up in one. He winks and says, "Merry Christmas." The bag is filled with items from the commissary that were confiscated from the naked prisoner: tobacco and coffee. He didn't have a receipt accounting for the purchased goods. I give a hollow thank you and head towards my office area with the bag, feeling like the driver of a get-away car at a robbery.

A few moments later, I pass another check-point. A guard is harassing a prisoner for smoking in a designated smoke-free zone. His master-speaking-to-slave tone shifts to dog-in-heat mode in a blink of an eye: a nurse walks by heading to the infirmary smoking a cigarette. Just as quickly, he is back as the overseer speaking to the field-hand, "Ya know smokin da masta's crops illega in dees here parts."

I round a bend and walk by the Adjustment Center on my right, better known as the AC. It's a squat block of a building, decorated with barred windows. The AC's hundred cells and four miniature yards—these prisoners' entire world— houses a hundred of California's most infamous prisoners. I don't know what kind of adjustments occur in the center, but the few prisoners who exit its gates often are headed to the infirmary, if not the morgue.

To my left are four prison chapels: Muslim, Jewish, Protestant, and Catholic. These neat, white painted buildings stand together facing the AC, giving me the impression of being spectators at a lynching. I've always found the proximity of these buildings symbolic. Now if I can only figure out who's praying for whom. Is society praying for the individual who's failed so miserably, or is it the other way around?

Through two swinging doors and I'm in a heated office where prisoner clerks are busy typing. I sit down at my word processor situated in the corner of the room and scan the handwritten infraction—possession of heroin. The hapless addict is facing an extra three months or a few years depending on whether the DA picks up his case.

I put on my walkman and begin transposing the handwritten text onto forms specific to the write-up charge. I'm hoping the music will take my mind off the role I have in giving another prisoner more time. It never helps. After every correction I make and every word I type, I become more and more ill. It's as if I've swallowed something abominable. Every time I partake in this feast, where the powerful eats the helpless, a part of me dies. I feel sorry for the nearby clerks who must see my agonizing countenance. I glance up and see my pain on all their faces.

The write-up completed, I exit the office and head around a bend and down a slope to the Squad's office. Climbing five steps, I press a buzzer and wait. A moment later a Nazi Stormtrooper appears in a CDC jumpsuit, collects my folder, and sends me off with an unholy grin. I now know how Dante felt leaving the ninth circle.

At the bottom of the steps, I stop and hang my head

in shame. To my left, the spot where George Jackson was murdered, I bow. I ask the Soledad brother to forgive a brother-in-spirit who's degraded himself by assisting in lengthening another prisoner's incarceration. My daily tug-o-war of principles against comfort continues: Am I compromising my beliefs? If I worked as a janitor in the prison infirmary or as a clerk in the Warden's office, wouldn't I still be assisting oppression? Comforts win again. Heading to the recreational yard to sweat the disgust off my body, a crisp wind bites through my state blues carrying with it a message from the dead, "Don't be too hard on yourself, lil' brother. Your time will come and when it does, you'll make me proud." I feel the shackles of imprisonment loosen on my limbs.

Floating by the first check point on an euphoric high, I see a guard shooing away two homosexual prisoners as if they're mangy mutts who'd gotten too close to him. The earth feels the dead weight of my body once again. Descending two flights of stairs to the yard, I find a vacant picnic table and take off my denim uniform, all the while thinking only flies and their unborn have picnics here.

A moment later a Nazi Stormtrooper appears in a CDC jumpsuit, collects my folder, and sends me off with an unholy grin. I now know how Dante felt leaving the ninth circle.

In sweat pants that I wear under my jeans, I run. I run from guilt. I run from reality. I run to escape. Thirty minutes later, I am on all fours almost retching from exhaustion. The taste of shame a little less sharp in my mouth, I grab a seat on a bench and watch demons chase other prisoners around the quarter-mile track.

My mind wanders. I hitch a ride with clouds drifting overhead. I see myself laying on their cottony softness, being transported to better times: I am in the uppermost compartment of a linen closet. Hiding behind sheets and towels, I find solace in smells of washed laundry and darkness.

A booming voice over the P.A. system pulls me away from

my childhood refuge. The yard is closed. I get dressed and shuffle back to the stairs with the rest of the herd, wondering if I will ever find peace in darkness again. At the top of the stairs I stop.

"Escooooort!" Death in handcuffs is flanked by flak-jacketed badges. I turn away from the condemned man and face the wall, mirroring the prisoners around me. I look to my left and see a young Hispanic man with tattoos adorning his neck and face, reading his life line in the cracks on the wall. To my right, a long-haired, bearded, white man, who reminds me of a short Jesus, is eyeing the ground, drooling—cigarette butts. I hand Jesus the brown bag filled with the loot that I've been carrying. He warily peeks inside then hugs the bag to his chest as if all his earthly possessions are contained in it. I wonder what I look like in their eyes. They probably see what I see every morning in my pocket size mirror toothpasted to the wall—my father, a veteran who lost his country, and his dreams.

After a decade of incarceration, I still don't understand the logic of having to turn away from death row prisoners who are escorted from one part of the prison to another. Maybe it's because the administrators don't want us non-condemned prisoners seeing the contagious, indestructible human spirit captured on their faces, that their chamber, chair, or needle is useless against such an opponent. Shifting slightly, I see the condemned man holding his legal work in hands handcuffed behind his back, being led to the law library around the next corner.

"Escoooort!"

Zombies scatter. There is a disciplined calmness in his walk and demeanor that triggers my memory. I've seen the same aura surrounding Buddhist monks in my homeland—right before they set themselves on fire. Or maybe the administrators don't want the condemned to see our faces. Since we are the ones who look like the walking dead, their misery wouldn't be as intense, knowing that we're all condemned when we're imprisoned.

Turning away from the burning monk, I melt into the stream of men heading back to the housing unit adjacent to the chow hall. The smell of tonight's meal is heavy in the air. I taste bile in my mouth. Ahead, the herd of men six abreast is bottle-necked at a doorway one and a half men wide. After a few minutes, I enter a bustling morgue.

There is a disciplined calmness in his walk and demeanor that triggers my memory. I've seen the same aura surrounding Buddhist monks in my homeland—right before they set themselves on fire.

Five tiers and two hundred and ten cells—originally built to hold one man but now accommodating two—stare me in the face. I'm reminded of a giant beehive where death has made his home. I follow the flow of inching rush-hour traffic around a corner and see the same monster—another five tiers and two hundred and ten cells. Finally, on the two foot wide stairs that I'm sure was a fire escape in a prior life, I ascend in single file along with the other hundred plus worker bees to our home.

There are men standing in front of their cells talking seriously, some laughing; others panhandling door to door for a fix of coffee or tobacco; many are showering and many still are dreaming in a Thorzine-influenced sleepwalk. The buzzing of eight hundred men is almost insanity-inducing. I can understand why every so often a new booty would climb the stairs to the fifth tier, and instead of stopping, continue over the railing, adding his silent scream to the cacophony for the last time.

When my father and our family crowded into the US embassy's gates during South Vietnam's collapse in 1975, I wonder if in his wildest nightmares, he imagined a future like this for his son. I wonder if he knew that by cheating his fate—sure imprisonment for his anti-Communist views—he may have angered the Gods to such a degree that now fate, crawling out of the shadows of time, finds my flesh much sweeter. I try to imagine what his life would've been like if he had stayed in Vietnam. Could it be much worse than my life now? I snort and laugh. After twenty-five years of Americanization, I still can't shake my cultural superstitions.

On the narrow tier I have to squeeze by two youngsters in deep conversation to get to my cell. "I would die for you, Homeboy!" I hear one say to the other. Gangster-bonding. Words I've lived by for much of my life. In hindsight, I recognize what a hollow truth that was. It's not that I wasn't willing to die for my homies—I was, and, in a sense, now serving a life sentence for killing a gang rival who threatened my homies— I am. No, it was the truth. The hollowness about it was that I was hollow. Under my silent and fearless exterior which I mastered by practicing the philosophy that men are like rocks—hard and emotionless—I was empty inside. It was as if a chain hung around my neck with a heavy medallion of nothingness attached to it. And instead of the chain resting on my chest, it sunk into my chest cavity, banging into ribs and organs, rattling with my every breath. I have the impulse to correct young Al Capone, "I would trade nothingness for you, Homeboy!" But I don't—gangster etiquette.

Once in my cell, I flip on the radio. As I peel down and get ready for my shower, I hear there's been another school shooting. I don't know if I'm more disgusted with the waste of human life or with the media circus sure to come afterwards. Probably the latter. The greater waste is when death becomes entertainment for the living. I can already hear the commentator's grave voice asking, "How can we as a community not see the signs leading up to this tragedy?" They should've used their ears instead of their eyes. The clink of chain and nothingness against ribs are unmistakable. Even under the maddening din of blaring speakers, slamming gates, screaming whistles and alarms, I can still recognize its hollow ring. It's most noticeable at night when I'm counting stars on a moonless ceiling and everyone's asleep. The ringing reminds me of chimes on the front porch of my childhood home. Coming home from elementary school, the house would be empty. And no matter where I went in the house, the farthest bedroom, I would hear those chimes ring. I'd close the door, go into the bathroom, close the door, but still would hear those chimes ringing. After a few years of coming home to emptiness, the ringing became a part of me.

Down the tier and a flight of steps and I'm at the watering hole. It's crowded: twenty-eight showerheads for eight hundred men. Fourteen showerheads are segregated for blacks, the other half for the rest of the population. The Old South is alive and well in California prisons. Cold air is blowing through a door twenty feet away and puddles of fouled water lay in wait on the ground—a fungus minefield. I wonder how many more of these showers must I endure to get clean? I hold my breath and submerge myself in inhumanity.

I get in and come out quickly. Not quickly enough. Someone has mistaken my towel and boxers that I've hung up for their own. I walk back to my cell naked and wet. In the cell while I'm toweling off, my name is blared through the loud speaker. I have a visit. I forgot this is the time of the month my parents pay their respects. My family has two altars for paying homage to dead family members. One is on the mantle above the fireplace at our home. The other is in the visiting room at my prison.

My mother fled her homeland to save her husband from imprisonment only to find imprisonment waiting for her son in America.

Mom and Dad are sitting at a knee-high table, hunched over vending machine food. They seem to be praying over the food like they do at home in front of the fireplace, bowing to pictures of my grandparents. Instead of the sharp scent of incense, cheap perfume chokes the air. They greet me with a smile that fails to reach their eyes. We sit and my Mom begins telling me about life being too hectic at her age; about trouble with the in-laws; about my nephew being old enough to walk and talk and ask why his uncle is in prison. I feel like a ghost listening to her thoughts as she kneels in front of the fireplace. Next to me, my dad sits silently eyeing the people around us who remind him of dead Americans he once knew in Viet Nam.

Two hours pass quickly. Visiting hours are over. We get

up and my Mom starts to cry. I hug her and am still amazed that her head only reaches my sternum. I wonder how a woman of her small stature can carry such enormous loads of suffering. She fled her homeland to save her husband from imprisonment only to find imprisonment waiting for her son in America. I stroke her trembling back, trying to soothe her pain, remembering the way she used to comfort me as a child: humming my favorite lullaby with her gentle hand through my hair. I hear the same lullaby and realize I'm humming to her. She looks up at me with tired eyes, telling me in tears that she's ready for her picture to be placed on our mantle, but holds off eternal peace until the return of her son.

My Dad pats me on the back repeating, "Hang in there. Hang in there." I look into his eyes and get the feeling that even though he's looking at me, he's addressing himself. It's as if he knows the life sentence I'm now serving should be his, and that if he survives his guilty conscience, then I will survive my sentence. I pull away and disappear in a sea of tears and farewells. In the strip out area, I wait in line to let a stranger look into my body cavities.

Back in my cell, I take my mind off my problems by reading a book of Neruda's. "Blood has fingers and it opens tunnels underneath the earth." How did a Chilean poet describe an experience that only a Viet Cong could know? Pondering yet another of life's ironies, I let Pablo's words, the clinking chimes, and the occasional toilet flushing, whisper me to sleep...

I'm in the back seat of a parked car. It's not a Datsun but a military jeep. There is no laughter, although Peter, June, and Tuna are in their usual places. Instead of leather jackets and dress slacks, we're wearing green military fatigues. A bead of sweat slithers down the back of my neck then down my spine, leaving goose bumps in its wake. There is fear in the air that is thicker than the sticky heat surrounding everything. This is not California. I'm wondering why Peter isn't leaving to buy beer when I realize we're not at a liquor store but a road block. I see a group of armed Vietnamese soldiers dressed in military fatigues, different from our own, approach our jeep. Something is definitely not right here, yet eerily familiar. My boys file out of the jeep and I'm about to do the same when the barrel of an AK-47 jabs into my chest, knocking me backwards onto the back seat. The barrel eases into the driver's side window and nods, "Remember me?" The words did not come from human lips. I have a picture of something that crawls on its belly and lives in shadows. In a voice not my own and filled with resignation, I answer, "Yes."

"BOOM!" An intense, burning pain digs into my chest. I look down and see to the left of a smoking hole, leaking blood, a name tag: Ông Già, my father's name. I look up and see my father's face staring back at me in the rear view mirror. I gag.

Bolting out of bed, I knee my locker and grab my throat, not wanting to swallow my tongue. On the P.A. system, a nasally, female voice is in the middle of a drawn out threat. ❖ ❖ ❖

Autobiography @ 33

Eddy Zheng

I am 33 years old and breathin'

it's a good year to die

to myself

I never felt such extreme peace

despite being mired in constant ear-deafening screams

from the caged occupants – triple CMS[1], PCs[2], gang validated,

        drop-outs, parole violators, lifers,
drug casualties, three strikers,
human beings

in San Quentin's 150 year old solitary confinement

I don't want to start things over

@ 33

I am very proud of being who I am

I wrote a letter to a stranger who said
    "You deserve to lose at least your youth,
    not returning to society until well into middle age…"

after reading an article about me in San Francisco Weekly

I told him
> "A hundred years from now when we no longer exist on
> this earth of humankind the seriousness of my crime will
> not be changed or lessened. I can never pay my debt
> to the victims because I cannot turn back the hands of
> time…I will not judge you."

whenever I think about my crime I feel ashamed

I've lost my youth and more

I've learned that the more I suffer the stronger I become

I am blessed with great friends

I talk better than I write

because the police can't hear my conversation

the prison officials labeled me a trouble maker

I dared to challenge the administration
for its civil rights violation

I fought for Ethnic Studies in the prison college program

I've been a slave for 16 years under the 13th Amendment

I know separation and disappointment intimately

I memorized the United Front Points of Unity

I love my family and friends

my shero Yuri Kochiyama and a young sister named Monica

who is pretty wanted to come visit me

somehow I have more female friends than male friends

I never made love to a woman

sometimes I feel like 16

but my body disagrees

some people called me a square

because I don't drink, smoke, or do drugs

I am a procrastinator but I get things done

I've never been back to my motherland

I started to learn Spanish

escribió una poema en español

at times I can be very selfish and vice versa

I've never been to a prom, concert, opera, sporting event

or my parents' house

I don't remember the last time I cried

I've sweat with the Native Americans, attended mass with the

Catholics, went to service with the Protestants, sat and chanted

with the Buddhists

my mind is my church

I am spoiled

in 2001 a young lady I love stopped loving me

it felt worse than losing my freedom

I was denied parole for the ninth time

I assured Mom that I will be home one day

after she pleaded me to answer her question truthfully

"Are you ever going to get out of prison?"

the Prison Industrial Complex and its masters attempted to
    control my mind

it didn't work

they didn't know I've been introduced to Che, Yuri Kochiyama,
Paulo Freire, Howard Zinn, Frederick Douglass, Assata Shakur,
bell hooks, Maurice Cornforth, Malcolm X, Gandhi, George
Jackson, Mumia, Buddha,

and many others…

I had about a hundred books in my cell

I was internalizing my politics

In 2000 I organized the first poetry slam in San Quentin

I earned my associate of art degree

something that I never thought possible

I've self-published a zine

I was the poster boy for San Quentin

some time in the '90s my grandparents died

without knowing that I was in prison

@ 30

I kissed Dad on the cheek and told him that I love him
for the first time

I've written my first poem

I called myself a poet to motivate me to write

because I knew poets would set us free

in 1998 I was granted parole

then it was taken away

the governor's political career superseded my life

some time in the 90s
I participated in most of the self-help programs

in 1996 I really learned how to read and write

I read my first history book "A People's History
of the United States"

my social conscious mind was awakened

in 1992 I passed my GED in Solano Prison

I learned how to take care of my body from '89 to '93

in 1987 I turned 18 and went to the Pen from youth authority

the youngest prisoner in San Quentin's
Maximum Security Prison

I was lucky people thought I knew kung fu

@ 16

I violated an innocent family of four and scarred them for life

money superseded human suffering

I was charged as an adult and sentenced to life
with a possibility

no hablo ingles

I wish I could start things over

I was completely lost

@ 12

I left Communist China to Capitalist America

no hablo ingles

I was spoiled

in 1976 I went to demonstrations against the Gang of Four

life was a blur from 1 to 6

on 5/29/69

I inhaled my first breath.

1 Correctional Clinical Case Management System Mental health
   condition of prisoners
2 Protective Custody of Prisoners

Prison

Untitled ◆ *Hyung-Rae,* (2004) ink on paper

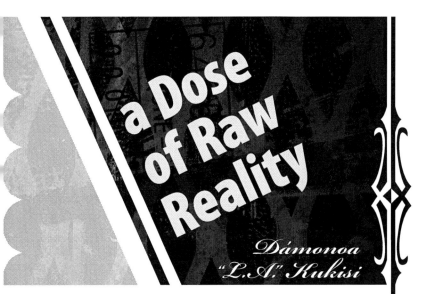

a Dose of Raw Reality

Dámonoa "L.A." Kukisi

INTRO

I am in prison for first degree attempted murder. Wow! What a charge! I say that because in law there are no degrees in an attempt, but yet in a flash, my lovely life had been taken and I was given a life sentence. Yeah, that's right. Life in prison. First offense, no criminal record, and no one died. Oh, did I mention I am a minority and he is not? At first, I wasn't the type to use that excuse as a crutch, but the more I experience it, the more I am haunted by the harsh realities of this environment. Yes, I was convicted, even though the evidence overwhelmingly proved to be in my favor. I know what you're thinking, so stop it now! I am not bitter, I'm just stating the facts and if my story can uplift a soul, then I'll gladly share it! So sit back and allow me to give you a small "Dose of Raw Reality".

Do not be deceived. Innocent people, and people who really don't deserve to, come to prison all the time. It's simply a matter of law structure, and brainwashing to believe that anyone who ends up as a defendant must be guilty.

An alarming number of Californians, mostly minorities, are either in prison, have been to prison, or have been to jail. An equally alarming number are either on parole or probation, or have been on parole or probation at one time in their lives. In fact, you would be hard pressed to find someone who does not either know someone incarcerated, or has been incarcerated before. California is a police state. That's a fact. The reality is the system is bursting at the seams. Every prison and county jail is overcrowded. This is indisputable. And this is just the way the devils like it.

MONEY vs REHABILITATION

Contrary to the misguided belief that the prison system is here to correct, incarcerate and rehabilitate, the truth is that corrections in California is about one thing - money. That's right. The massive budget crisis in the State of California in recent years has resulted in deep cuts in everything from education, emergency services, public safety, and health care. However, the biggest department in California made no deep cuts - the California Department of Corrections and Rehabilitation (CDCR). In fact, in the midst of the budget crisis, the prison guards received a raise. While teachers, firefighters and emergency medical technicians were getting pink slips from their jobs; while libraries and schools were closing, Correctional Officers were receiving a raise in pay. Pull into the parking lot of any institution, and you will see Hummers, Escalades, Navigators, and Mercedes Benzs' - all belonging to prison guards. Go figure. Of course, the only budget cuts made to the prisons were to the inmate programs that keep peace within the prisons - visiting (needed to create positive family and community ties) and programs geared towards rehabilitation.

Learning in prison, at one time, was exciting, and offered a wide variety of options for the inmate. There were enough trade programs to allow every inmate the opportunity to learn marketable skills so that they would have a greater chance of success when they returned to society. Things have definitely changed. Today, the trade programs have been reduced to almost nothing. And the reasoning from the administration, is that there is a budget crisis. This

California is a police state. That's a fact. The reality is the system is bursting at the seams. And this is just the way the devils like it.

is an oxymoron - the Department of Corrections and Rehabilitation provides no rehabilitation. How can this be a Corrections and Rehabilitation Department, but barely provide any programs to correct and rehabilitate?

Because education is so important for survival in society, one would think that the CDCR would place a high priority, not just in word, but in deed on inmates having the best opportunity to survive on the outside, seeing that this would prevent them from victimizing others. But alas, it does not work like that. Education is a joke in prison. Inmates are discouraged from learning. Despite what you may have been told, the prison officials do not want to see an inmate succeed. Why? Because that would reduce the constant influx of bodies that the prison guards union relies upon. In order to keep the business running properly, a constant influx of new bodies is required. Therefore, it would be foolish to believe that the system would ever want anyone rehabilitated and released. Keeping the individual incarcerated for life is highly profitable for those who run the Department of Corrections.

The current laws in California, developed by a Legislature that is controlled by the prison guards union, were created to keep the system full. The politicians are willing to be lobbied because they are receiving large amounts of money, gifts and vacations from the prison guards union. The more crime, the more prisons are needed. The more prisons, the more guards are needed. More guards means more money for the union. And more money for the union means more kickbacks to the politicians. To hell with the lives that are destroyed. With facts like these, is there any wonder why California has the largest prison system in the world? It is now even larger than those in third world countries that have literally no judicial system.

REHABILITATION, REAL OPPORTUNITY

For a person to become truly reformed, "they must perceive real hope of success as a law-abiding citizen." Understand, for those who have spent much time in prison, the mind set, pertaining to society, is that no one really wants them out there. No one will give them a "real" chance. Thus, they end up staying on the path that they know best. It's not that they like it in prison. It's just that they do not know what else to do. Understand that!

So, what is a "real" opportunity? It is a chance at a decent job. Not one that will keep a person permanently below the poverty level. An opportunity to better themselves, and their standard of living. Not only for themselves, but also for their families. Remember, it is common sense to see that most crimes are committed because of poverty.

In truth, the average criminal is a regular person who for whatever reason fell off the path of society's norm, and into a counter-culture that has provided whatever a person was missing in their lives. Once a person is exposed to prison, they become mentally ill, and caught up in the system. The one thing that most inmates have in common, is that they are pessimistic. They do not see a bright future as a citizen. They need optimism. And that is achieved through "real" opportunity. Personally, I have been around thousands of criminals, and contrary to popular belief, most are not the rabid dogs, and drug-crazed psychopaths that they have been portrayed to be.

Once the average inmate is released, after being programmed to see themselves as nothing, and unwanted by society, they are constantly faced with the reality that the majority will not allow them to rise above their past. The present cycle of destroying human lives can be changed, if only you have a change of heart, soul, and mind. Start by

Contrary to popular belief, most are not the rabid dogs, and drug-crazed psychopaths that they have been portrayed to be.

seeing the situation for what it is - that a person who has been separated from society must be repaired mentally, as well as physically. To get the ex-offender's mind right, it starts in prison through "real" rehabilitation programs focused on successful reintegration into society.

The next step, is on you. The prevailing attitude in society must be one of acceptance, and encouragement. This is shown by no longer denying the ex-offender decent employment, decent housing, a chance to purchase dependable transportation and, if necessary, advanced vocational on-the-job training. Most who come out of prison have families to support. They don't really have the option of forsaking a job for further education. It is important to keep in mind that although they went astray, ex-offenders are still human beings. Of course, as with every other facet of life, there will be failure. Not everyone who comes out of prison and receives an equal opportunity will succeed. There will be backsliding. However, the point is society needs to do their part in at least giving these men and women a fighting chance.

Despite being beat down mentally and emotionally by those who benefit financially from human cargo, the average inmate will indeed embrace and flourish after being offered real opportunity to succeed.

WHAT IS TO BE DONE

Accountability has now also come upon you, the public-at-large. You know the prison system is broken. You know that there is no actual rehabilitation going on. You know that billions of dollars are being wasted on keeping people in prison for life that should not be. You know where the cash cow is. Now the time has come for you to finish it off. The time is now for you to tear yourself away from the orbit of the CDCR, since it is not showing itself to be an asset by its current philosophy and its actions. Instead, it has proven to be a grave liability to public interest overall.

There is a way to cut the CDC giant down to size. It begins by your demand for change, and expectation that the change will not take decades. This can only happen when you have a change in your own thought, word and deed in providing those who come out of prison with a real opportunity to succeed on the outside, and never re-offend.

Demand and expect the implementation of real rehabilitation programs. Even if it means that a large number of nonviolent inmates are released, and some prisons are closed. God knows, we have more than enough of them. In fact, more than any nation on earth. You can demand that inmates receive competent medical treatment. And that inmates are allowed to keep their family and community ties strong through regular visiting and family visiting for both long- and short-term inamtes. Encourage the humanization of inmates and parolees, rather than ex-communication and ostracizing. As a people, it is time to advance just as much in our thinking as we do in technology.

You have the power to stop this state from becoming one big prison system. Lord knows that it is close already. Remember, the one thing politicians fear more than the prison guards' union, is the voters. A dose of raw reality is what is needed today. You need to know that as long as you allow yourself to be led into supporting a bigger prison sytem and draconian laws over education, you are supporting the greater chance that someone in your family, or circle of friends will end up incarcerated. Yes, even you! ◆ ◆ ◆

I Want People to Know

Hemnauth Mohabir

(Detained at Passaic County Jail – New Jersey)

Hello. Greetings to all. This is Hemnauth Mohabir, speaking out about the Passaic County Jail in New Jersey. There is so much we can say about the food, the building structure, the… supply system, the carbon monoxide smell in the dorm, the leaks in the room, the shakedown with the dogs, the roaches, and so on. But my main concern in the jail is the system and the abuse by officers on the detainees.

This January, detainees were conducting a hunger strike, writing letters to get out, trying to get transferred to other jails and stuff like that. On July 16, after conducting 16 days of hunger strike, a sergeant and one conductor came and told me to pack up my shit because I'm going back into the dorm - "no more hunger strikes." They refused to keep me isolated, but I refused to go in the dorm where the other detainees were eating. The sergeant grabbed me, and told me, "Hey, you are going in there man." And then he grabbed me by my neck, swung me into the wall, and dragged me into the dorm. I was weakened, my feet were shaking, and I didn't have much strength. I fell to the ground, and when I came into the dorm, he pushed me over. Then he stood on top of a table and said, "No more hunger strikes. See what happens when you go on hunger strike?" He used what he did to me to intimidate the other guys in the dorm.

In March, the detainees conducted another hunger strike. I was a part of it also, when a friend of mine got beaten up by the police. In the night they came with the dog and they started beating him up. The dog jumped on him, but they claimed that he assaulted the dog. I got two punches in my rib, and they tore up all the bags and flushed it, our t-shirts, and our towels down the toilet bowl. They laughed and ran away. We made a complaint to the INS, but they never moved us. And they keep assaulting other people – stuff like that.

So I just want people to know what goes on in this place. People are losing their civil rights in this country, you know. You can get a charge for attempted possession of a weapon, or attempted sale of a controlled substance. That means that there is no evidence; there is no gun or no drug. But you can still get a charge once the policeman says that you "attempted to posses something." A charge like that could bring you into the INS custody, although they have no evidence. And they can still lock you up into the system. But people need to stand up against this injustice and demonic behavior, because it is spreading like a contagious disease. As time goes by, more and more people will be affected by it, you know what I mean? People keep coming in here all the time on petty charges and for stupid reasons. And the INS doesn't know when you are coming out and you get lost in the system. People are here for seven years and all that, trying to get results from the INS. Nigel is waiting for his appeal and he's been waiting on the results for two years now, you know what I mean. So the system now needs to be going in a different direction.

Alright, peace and love, thank you very much. ✦ ✦ ✦

Untitled ◆ *Hyung-Rae*, ink on paper

Human Rights

Anonymous South Asian Detainee

(Detained at Passaic County Jail – New Jersey)

We, the detainees, have deep sympathy and sorrow for the victims of September 11th and believe that the culprits should receive justice.

If we, who are locked in prison unjustly, have sympathy for the innocents who were killed, why do the American people not have sympathy for the victims jailed by the INS?! There are men here fifty and sixty years old, locked in small rooms, who have not breathed fresh air in four months. They are charged with no crimes. This is a violation of their human rights!

About three weeks ago, in the middle of the night, ten prison guards came into our dormitory with dogs. They pulled our roommate out of his bed and made him face the wall. They proceeded to kick him and punch him. They hit his head several times. When one of us spoke out to protest, they let the dog loose on that person too. One week later, the man who was severely beaten was gone – deported!

If this country allows this kind of injustice, how can it talk about human rights?! All innocent people are innocent – whether we are Asian, Arab, Christian or Muslim. There is no difference. We were innocent yesterday, today and will still be innocent tomorrow. But this country has now made us guilty until proven innocent. All we ask is that we should at least be allowed to leave this country with dignity. ✦ ✦ ✦

Hunger Strike

Anonymous
South Asian
Detainee

(*Detained at Wackenhut Correctional Facilities –*
New York)

I've been detained in these facilities, Wackenhut Correctional
Facilities for the last two years. I've undergone a lot of
traumatizing moments in my life. My case was denied without
reason by the judge. I'm just praying to God right now for the
outcome of my case. I'm so scared because I don't know what
the outcome is gonna be. I just want the government to look
deep into this case and do something about it. I entered the
United States of America to seek refuge because of persecution
in my country, but I get here and find myself being locked up
for this hell of a long time. I pray that we can get our freedom
in the United States.

Our hunger strike started Wednesday, because we wanted
to express how bad it is for us. This is the only way we can
express ourselves so the people outside may know about this
place. Now the press is talking about the hunger strike. We
need the people to push the government to give us freedom
and not keep us here. They keep me here like a criminal; this
place is supposed to be for criminals, not for immigrants.
I repeat it many times to everyone, "This place is only for
criminals." They scare us by threats to transfer us to another
prison, far away from here. We have nothing to do except

the hunger strike and some people stopped because they were scared by the transfer. We need some help from the outside.

During eight days here, the hunger strike continued because nobody could get any information. In New Jersey, I have an uncle – I need to speak to my uncle but they don't give any information. We've been here for one and a half years and don't have information. We don't have anything. We can't go to the doctor. We can't go to medical care and they don't give us referrals. They don't give anything. Most of the people here have five or seven years. Most of the people here are on the hunger strike. Many of the people, 8 or 9 people, are Sri Lankan too, and they are also on hunger strike. They have five years here. I can't go to Sri Lanka because it is having too much trouble. If you go back there is also killing. Nobody here gives any parole, bond or anything. I don't know why they keep people for so long a time.

We want to go, and have freedom. We are refugees, not criminals. We want to go outside. We don't get any sleep, there is so much sadness. ✦ ✦ ✦

Torture

Anonymous
South Asian
Detainee

(Detained at Passaic County Jail – New Jersey)

All I can say about this jail, is that it is the lowest standard of treatment a human being can get. After having been here for almost three months, I can face any kind of torture in the world. People are beaten here quite frequently—they are beaten for nothing. Many are beaten for refusing to eat food that is not halal because they are Muslim. Others are beaten and charged for praying by using their bed sheets as prayer rugs.

I have always been an open-minded person. My wife and I are here legally to study and felt we could move to the U.S. for its opportunities. But after these past few months, we never want to return. America is NOT a free country for certain people anymore—it is NOT a free country if you are Muslim. Stop detaining Muslims.

The Department of Justice should look deeply at its policies to judge whether what it is doing to Muslims is right. If we must leave, let us leave with dignity and respect instead of treating us like animals. Our main demand is this: Either let us go on bail or deport us immediately. Do not let us sit in cages forever for having committed no crimes. ✦ ✦ ✦

(This man was a Canadian resident legally in the U.S., arrested for sending tuition money to his wife while being Muslim.)

Living in a Cage

Anonymous Female Detainee

I have been missing home a lot since I came to the United States. It feels like a dream…things are so different now. Certainly, language is one big factor. I am feeling numb now as time passes. I have been thinking much about my adolescent time: happy, cheerful and carefree. Well, I understand that we ought to grow up one day, however.

I came here illegally when I became an adult and am now detained. I have been living the life of a bird that has no freedom; it's like living in a cage. A bird with freedom can fly anywhere it wishes, unlike me. Life is like a movie: I am enacting the life of a very miserable person, yearning for freedom and release. My dear friends, despite my situation, I have learned a lot that a person with freedom would never have learned; I have experienced a lot of challenges that a person with freedom would never have experienced.

I believe that there will be one day that I will be released. I need to be strong and continue to tolerate and endure. I have thought about banging my head against the wall so to kill myself as I have lost all my hope after my two years' of detention here. My friends here were able to convince me otherwise and now I am able to live till today. To be honest, the saying, "we rely on our parents when we are home and we rely on our friends when we are away" has a lot of truth in it.

"自从来到美国之后 很怀念 它乡. 所有的事情都像做梦一样. 变了很多. 当然 就连语言都不一样了. 但是时间长了. 也就麻木了. 未成年的生活真是爽, 开心, 快乐的童年生活. 但是人总要长大. 成年了. 由于非法进入美国, 被关监狱过着像鸟一般的生活." 没有自由的鸟, 被关在笼子里. 失去了所有. 有自由的鸟呢. 则是在自由的空中飞翔. 想. 去哪. 就去哪. 唉. 人生就像一场戏, 现在的情况 就像是自己在饰演一个悲惨生活的戏角. 期待着得到解放和自由. 亲爱的朋友们, 虽然如此. 但是我学到了很多自由的人没有想到. 没有经历过的风霜. 相信会苦尽甘来的 终有一天 我们会被释放, 只要坚强. 振作起来. 坚持到底. 我之前也曾想过. 时间都就天了要两年了. 还没有结果. 当时的我想. 要去撞墙自杀. 放弃了希望. 但身边的朋友说服了我. 让我坚持到现在. 说真的 "在家靠父母, 出门靠朋友" 这句话挺有道理可言的. 如果没有朋友的支持, 帮助 和鼓励之下, 我想我现在不会在这等待着希望和机会的到来了. 这一次出国. 或是得到不少知识. 也让我学了不少的英语. 年也喜欢英语. 在中国没有认真学. 现在我要把握机会. 同时也很高兴认识很多收容所的朋友 和老师们 同时很感激老师们教我的一些知识. 并且认识了神. 这么一来我就更加地希望能留在美国, 去做所不知道的事. 当然是指好方面. 在美国, 有很多犯罪的人被关. 比任何地方想. 像都比较严格. 所以希望朋友们要遵守法律. 少犯罪."

If I didn't have the support and encouragement of friends, I wouldn't still have the hope that I might have the opportunity to be set free one day. In addition, I have gained quite a lot of knowledge now that I am away from home. I have learned quite a bit of English also. I like English. I didn't have a chance to really practice it when I was in China.

Now I am making use of this opportunity. At the same time, I am happy that I have met many friends and teachers here and very much appreciate the knowledge that they give me. I have also come to known more about God. I still have a strong wish that I can stay in the United States so I can try many different things and, of course, I mean good things. There are many strict rules in detention here in the United States. I hope that you all will obey the laws and stay away from crimes. ✦ ✦ ✦

English translation: Wing Yee Wong

Amelioration of Dilapidation

P. J. R.

It's finally here
The long awaited 2004
Many years lost
I'm 25 years old
16 years of callow life
9 years squandered
Will I recognize the world?

The sands of time persisted
While I waited in idle isolation
Life's milestones elapsed
No senior prom or graduation
Sentenced on my 18th birthday
10 years, 85 percent
Turned 21 in the hole
Transition to manhood spent in solitude

A puerile teen tried as an adult
Not fit for juvenile court
According to my file
From juvenile hall to Tracy[1]

Thrown into a three tier building of wolves
Learned the guidelines of prison politics
Consigned to Corcoran
Level 3 inmate on a level 4 yard[2]
No bed space for "others"
Riots, stabbings, and death in my periphery
200 miles away from home
No visits, no money for canteen

No girlfriend, no friends left

The road ahead seemed arduous
Constant anguish
Covert struggles within
A lost soul wandering
Aimlessly through life

My future a nebulous haze
Until a spontaneous turning point
Agony, misery, and tribulation
Concocted into perplexity
Spirit responded like a chemical reaction
An exigent wake up call
A phase of protracted intuition
A subconscious prophecy
Of my own fate

Too inundated with adversity
To realize this florescence
That took place internally
A prolonged epiphany
Extricated my soul
Freed my mind
Opened my eyes
I finally understand life
I see the world clearly
Drafted blueprints of my destiny
Like a butterfly's metamorphosis
I sit here in a cocoon
The old me eradicated
Three months until I hatch
Begin a new life
Spread my wings and fly
With every intention to fulfill
My limitless dreams
Ameliorate my dilapidated life

---

1   *A prison of California's penal system*
2   *California prisons are divided into four custody levels, level 4 being*
    the highest

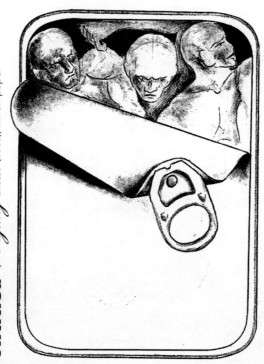

Untitled ✦ *Hyung-Bae* (2005), ink on paper

Unforgettable Experience

Đạt Nguyễn

I step off of the police car and walk towards the entrance of Juvenile Hall. It is four hours after the cops rushed inside of my home and took me to County to book me in as an adult, but they are housing me in the Hall because I am underage. Nods and smiles as heads shake. "What can I do?" A female counselor at police admissions asks the officer. "Nothing much. He's all yours," the cop answers. "Three counts of attempted murder. A big one this time Mr. Nguyen," she says, as she flips through my rap sheet. Too tired to answer, I shrug my shoulders with sarcasm.

It is about 4:30 am on a Thursday morning, May 11, 2004, the day after my birthday. I stand against the wall waiting for a mug shot. I'm wearing sweats with slippers and three hats stacked on top of each other on my head that the cop picked-out of my closet. "Happy 16th birthday, Đạt," the counselor says with sarcasm as she writes down my charges, adding onto many others that I had picked up over the years.

The officer then proceeds to un-cuff me. I take off the hats and try to slick my hair back for the mug shot. I'm too tired to pose for a tough guy look. It is blurry, like a bad dream that I wish I would wake up from. After the police admission process, I walk to Boys Receiving (BR), another familiar process.

"What's up, Đạt!?" the male counselor in BR greets me. "Man!" He sighs as he turns and looks at me after he reads the charges. I shrug my shoulders and begin to strip. He gives me a bag to throw my clothes in and he hands me county-issued clothes. I walk toward the shower and close the dirty green curtain behind me. The ice-cold water hits me like needles, but I am used to it. When I hit the pump on the soap bottle, I get a wake up call. It is that same old, yellow soap that we use for everything.

As I am dialing my home number for my first phone call, I feel ashamed putting my parents in this situation once again. My dad picks up the phone and mumbles a few words. Then I hang up the phone. I sit there and start to think the whole night over: about my charges, about my homeboys, about the police kicking in my door, about the room I was sitting in, and how the Hall smells of bad body odor and the stench of wine.

I pick up my roll, which consists of two sheets and a blanket, and walk out of BR with the counselor who has to escort me. I was an SR-1 (Security Risk 1), which meant I could not walk out of the unit without being escorted by a counselor. I was a threat to the main population. I walked down that hall so many times before, but never so early in the morning. It was quiet; too quiet without all the movement. The counselor yells, "B8!" as we pass by control.

We entered B8, a unit that I would end up living in for the next two-plus years, where I've lived in time after time in all but three cells, where I've had fights in almost all areas, where I've met so many good people and a few scandalous ones, where I earned my high school diploma, where I'm going to stay until I'm old enough for state prison, and where I grew up on the nonsense around me.

I came into B8 with nothing to lose. I was facing triple life for something that I did not do. When counselors advised me to calm down, I laughed. Life was getting worse by the moment, set-trippin' on everyone I met. Fights and IRs (Incident Reports) didn't phase me. I refused to let the

You gangbang on the street earning a rep... but when you get in the Pen, there's nothing like that. They don't like that street bullshhh here.

mentality go. Nobody could tell me nothing. It all went out one ear and out the other. Back then to me, I couldn't let all the dirt I put in go away. I was there for something I didn't do, something I was down to get life for. No regrets, it's the game that we play. I didn't want to move on with my life.

My first year was spent mostly in my cell. I couldn't last with a regular program (A and B level) for more than two weeks until I picked up a fight or something to go back to C level, but mostly C-mod. I've been to isolation cell in BR so many times, I've been to it all. The PO from gang task force would come and try to scare me, but they got laughed at because I was charged as an adult. I was heading for the Pen.

Many counselors tried to help me, even when I messed up. During those years, it was Mr. Montgomery in the morning and Mr. Crockett at night. It wasn't that I couldn't get help, it was that I didn't want help. I didn't want to help myself.

I got tired of that fast, as I do with everything else. Staying in the cell watching the guys program - it wasn't that I couldn't stand staying in the cell, it was just boring for me. I'm an active person and excitement wasn't in the room.

It was around shift change of 2001. They were going to reassign a whole new staff to the unit. Mr. Crockett and Mr. Montgomery was really good to me, but many other staff there had grudges against me because I fought on their shift and one of them couldn't, after many attempts, write me up and give me extra charges that I sure didn't need, so I decided maybe when the new staff members come, I would try a fresh start with them.

Right before the shift change, my homeboys got into it

with the other gang. The day after the phase (riot), one of my homies tried to stab the other guy. When new staff members came in, they wanted to make an example (a statement). They shut the program down. After a few weeks, we programmed slowly. For the first time, something happened and I wasn't involved. Me and the other homies were out in the courtyard playing handball.

I started to act right. I started to worry about my case instead of set-trippin'. As I programmed and worried about my business and not about anyone else's, my time started to go by easy. Ms. Bishop, Mr. McKelton, Mr. Logan, Mr. Birchard, Mr. Navarro, Mr. Sullivan, Mr. Reyes, and Ms. Soria all helped me out in so many different ways. It was the easiest time I've done so far.

So I waited for my fate to unfold and waited for my transfer to the State Pen. My eyes started to open. I'm glad now that I did that. When I started to program, I focused on school and I got my diploma. I got things I didn't know I could get. I didn't have to worry about watching my back, not that I don't anymore.

I realized that I was just taking the homies' places that were before me. I laid on beds that many laid on before. It's just a vicious cycle that'll keep going on unless we educate our little brothers and sisters, homeboys and homegirls. The sad thing is that as soon as I left, many of you lined up to take my place, and many want to take your place, and it goes on. I called it (B8) my home, yet it was just a unit and cells in it. Nothing lasts forever. Soon, we all got to go on with our lives.

We all got to go on with our life. There's too much to do on the streets other than gang bangin'. Trust me, even guys I've met in here with their sets tattooed on their heads told me that. If you get out soon, then good. Even if you're facing life, you have too much to worry about to be doing all that. Stand up for you and be proud of where you're from. I'm not knocking no one's 'hood, set, or side, but play it smart. You gangbang on the street earning a rep, putting in work, and taking penitentiary chances, but when you get in the Pen, there's nothing like that. They don't like that street bullshhh here. You stay with your people and treat everyone with respect or else. You represent where you are from, but watch what you say or how you say it.

We're all different, yet in so many ways we're all the same. My homies and I in the Hall were like brothers before I left. We saw each other as homies once we looked past the tattoos on each other. I was there with guys who I had fought with when we first arrived, but we ended up cellies before I left. We do so much damage to each other on the streets, we should come together to fight the system together. We don't have to become best of friends, but we need to have a mutual ground where we understand each other's program. For all we know, we can be each other's cellie in the Pen someday.

To all the homies in the Hall, especially B8 and B9, just enjoy your time. Penitentiary time or not, we have too much to do and worry about. Always remember where you come from, but don't let your pride hold you down. Listen to the wise words that come your way. Soak it in, don't shut it out. Nobody is perfect. Your mentality (way of thinking) will always stay with you. It's a part of you, but it is up to you to keep it in check and know what will be good for your future. Work on bettering yourself mentally, physically, and intellectually.

Remember if you're going home, there's too much to do out there other than taking penitentiary chances. You don't want to go to the Pen to realize it. If you're heading to the Pen, there's too much for you to worry about other than set-tripping. There's a long road ahead. Plan out what you want to do with your time. You should enjoy being at home and take advantage of it by getting your diploma or GED since you're at home. More days will become brighter once you allow yourself to shine.

I wrote this from experience.
Much respect from this end. ✦ ✦ ✦

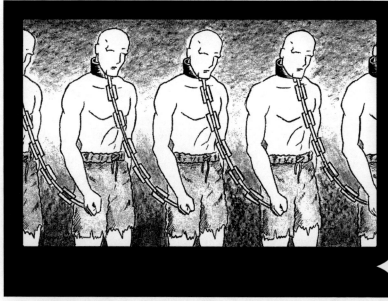

Untitled ✦ *Hyung-Rae*, ink on paper

the Slave Mentality

Dámonoa "L.A." Kukisi

As I sit in this cage that houses me, mulling over the latest round of slander being spread about me behind my back, I am reminded of the power of the slave mentality that dominates the lives of the majority of prison inmates, and how it is trained to persecute any insurrectionist seeking to erase it.

Long ago, slave plantations served as places where people were oppressed and persecuted. While on the plantation, they were beat down and trodden underfoot until many became happy to be a slave and came to love their master - even more than their own families on many occasions.

Today, the equivalent of those bygone plantations are American prisons. In particular, the California prison system and the slaves come in all colors; predominantly minorities. Of which, as a Pacific Islander, I am considered to be.

As with every other minority inmate, I was thrown in prison and expected to just vegetate. The concept of rehabilitation is nothing more than a myth, since California operates from an unwritten edict of "no parole." It is the Master's belief that everyone in prison is dumb in one way or another. Therefore, they should be content as wards of the state. But, whenever that rare one comes along who attempts to enlighten the people by thinking outside of the box, he is viewed as a threat, and thus discredited among his peer group.

Within the confines of prison, there are few opportunities for a man to rise above his circumstance and see himself as more than just an inmate. One such activity involves inmate fundraising.

As the president of the Asian/Pacific Islander activity group, I conducted a fundraiser that garnered the most money in the history of prison activity groups.

True to form, when prison officials saw the amount of money raised, and realized that they had agreed to receiving none of the proceeds, like a ravenous wolf, they wanted a cut. To do this, they put an immediate freeze on the funds raised. Their next move was to falsely accuse me of attempting to steal money – and then threw me in the hole.

The truth is that all of the proceeds from the fundraiser was to go to minority charities. And the prison was not going to get any money. So in order to get a piece of the pie, they did what they do best. They deceived the people in believing that I was up to no good. Afterward, it was easy to tear the house down. They cancelled the fundraiser first. They gave everyone their money back. They then negotiated with another inmate activity group (one that would give them a portion of the proceeds) to conduct the fundraiser; gave them all my contacts, and conducted the event again. In other words, they stole my work by accusing me of attempting to do something slick. All the while, they were the one being slick.

Nevertheless, among the general population, the vicious lies about me led to disparaging rumors that were detrimental to my well being. My life was placed in danger all because some horny little devil wanted to steal the money I raised.

After walking through this valley of death for over a decade, I was not surprised by the deceptive tactics of the system. What did surprise me, however, was how ingrained the slave mentality is in the minds of my beloved brothers. I had lived in harmony with many of them for years, and I have always been there to help any of them in their time of need. But as soon as Master put out his poison, they forgot all that they knew about me and turned like spoiled milk.

No words can express the disappointment and hurt that I feel even now. Not because of the backbiting, but because of the blindness of my people. And how easy it is for Master to get them to turn on one of their own. Their minds could not conceive that I was being set up.

Typical of a defeated and subjugated people, my brothers refuse to overcome and rise above their condition. As long as they have temporary prison trinkets such as sneakers, televisions, and coffee, they are content in a condition of physical, mental, and spiritual bondage, and ready to down anyone who Master says is a threat to their crumbs.

How can we every truly overcome when material items are given a higher place in our lives than self-respect, unity, and loyalty to each other, and to the cause?

What makes the pain of the events I have spoken on in this piece drill to the bone, is the fact that although I was exonerated of all the false charges and released from the hole, many of my brothers still harbor ill-feelings towards me in silence. They remain under Master's spell.

As for myself, I am a soldier. I will continue to push my people to overcome. Even if I have to drag them kicking and screaming. We do not have to always be the tail. We can be the head, and uplift our individual communities. So I will continue to work to change the psychology of my brothers in bondage. And pray that one day they will stand on the path to righteousness and renaissance. ✦ ✦ ✦

Lesson Learned in Prison College

Việt Mike Ngo

There's an academic program at San Quentin State Prison (SQ) that's the only one of its kind: an Associate of Arts accredited, volunteer-run college. Professors and teaching assistants volunteer from nearby UC Berkeley, UC Davis, and Saint Mary's College; prisoners participate voluntarily as well.

In 2002, the warden of SQ, Jeanne Woodford, was hailed by the San Francisco Chronicle as a "new generation of wardens" for being at the helm of the only prison in the California Department of Corrections (CDC) to have a volunteer college. Other media outlets ran stories lauding the program for educating prisoners at no expense to taxpayers. The cover of a local paper showed the program's first three graduates – a black, white, and Asian prisoner, bedecked in cap and gown, huddled in a smiling embrace – an image of racial harmony that normally eludes prison settings.

I was a student in this program from its inception in 1996 until 2002 and can attest to its educational benefits. My writing skills progressed greatly and I've especially grown in my understanding of the American democratic process. It was my first Ethnic Studies class in this program that helped raise my consciousness regarding racial segregation and its impact on our society. But as praiseworthy as the program was, there was room for improvement. Myself and a small group of prisoner-students decided to apply what we've learned by submitting a proposal listing a number of suggested changes which we felt would enhance the program.

We requested that the decision-making process concerning classes taught and who teaches them be more inclusive; that a student body committee and one veteran volunteer be created to facilitate this process. We specifically asked for more Ethnic Studies classes due to demand from volunteer Professors and prisoner-students.

We disagreed to plans of corporate sponsorship without first seeking or receiving input from the student body and objected to the local prison policy that prohibited correspondence between prisoners and volunteers, citing that it violated prison regulations as well as the First Amendment.

Shortly after prison administrators received our proposal, Woodford initiated an investigation on the five signees. Of the five, three were Asians. Rico Remeidio, Eddy Zheng, and myself were placed in solitary confinement (the hole) pending the completion of their investigation.

While I was in the hole, the Marin Independent Journal ran a cover story about my petition of habeas corpus alleging SQ of practicing illegal racial segregation for which the Marin County Superior Court ordered an evidentiary hearing to resolve.[1] I had filed this petition shortly before the proposal submission. Three days later I was transferred to New Folsom, a maximum security prison, where I was admitted to a psychiatric ward within a solitary confinement unit.

Nearly two months and an interrogation later, I was returned back to SQ's hole where I was informed that the initial allegations against me that I was planning a violent take-over of Marin County's Courthouse during my upcoming evidentiary hearing were dropped. However, I was notified I faced a number of administrative charges regarding my involvement in the college program.

*I*t was my first Ethnic Studies class in this program that helped raise my consciousness regarding racial segregation and its impact on our society.

The Hearing Officer who adjudicated the charges dismissed all counts except one: corresponding with a volunteer, a non-serious offense. He found me guilty despite stating in his disposition that such correspondence appears to be allowed by prison regulations.

Prison officials informed me that the four month-long investigation, six months of solitary confinement, and five transfers was due to a non-serious, suspect, prison write-up for writing letters and not because of the proposal submission. My parole hearing was delayed over a year without my consent and when I did appear, I was denied two years, in part, for being the subject of Woodford's investigation, an experience I anticipate at future parole hearings.

Rico Remeidio, who had earned a parole date after twenty years of imprisonment, had his date rescinded, then given a year denial the following year on top of his four months of solitary confinement and transfer.

Eddy Zheng spent nearly a year in the hole, was transferred and received a year parole denial for his part in the proposal submission.

Jeanne Woodford received a promotion. She's now the Director of the CDC.

More than three years have passed since I've taken my last class in SQ's college program, yet my understanding of the American democratic process continues to grow. ✦ ✦ ✦

---

[1] *Although the Marin County Superior Court denied my petition, the US Supreme Court in another case, Johnson v. California et al., 543 U.S. ___(2005), has declared that CDC's racial segregation policies are suspect, overruling Marin's standard of review in my petition.*

Love & Fam

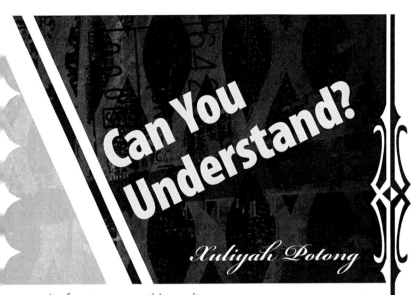

Can You Understand?

Xuliyah Potong

I refuse to accuse this result
As being the product of indifference from society
No fault lies in the possession of my father
My mother blessed me
With all the virtues that are apparent
In my essence today
I labor under the burden
Of accepting responsibility
For my late transgressions
I make no excuses
I am a man

All I want is for you to understand

Dearest Mama
Please do not be afraid
Independence means you are
No longer subjected to his abuse
Not that you are alone
Sister and I, will help you
Raise us
I am so fortunate
That you do not comprehend fully
The ways of this foreign world
That your love
Impairs your sight

Of the biased perception you have
Of me
For nothing else in existence
Could hide the adulterated butterfly
I have become
Your graceful presence
For an eternity
Will be mourned
Thank you celestial Father
For closing her eyes
Before she could witness
What has befallen her child

She would not understand

Dearest Papa
I am proud of you
For slaying the monster
That manifested itself
Through your indelible
Atrocities
If you did not leave
Redemption could not be achieved
Relieve yourself
Of the regret
That is so evident in your eyes
This is something I had to endure
Were it not for this
How else could I be
The serene spirit that
I am today
I wandered along the rugged
Edge of the cliff
And stumbled
But my fist is firmly clenched
On the branch of enlightenment
I will rise!
And no longer wallow
In the pungent decay of this cycle
Generations ago
After disrespecting myself
By mistreating you
You lovingly prophesied that
Although at present I fail to understand

One day
A coup
Will precipitate
A revolution within my being

I finally understand

Dear Mr. Governor
I was rebellious and impressionable
Allowing these defective traits in humanity
To overwhelm my compassion
Consequently
The judge decided against throwing away the key
He entrusted it to you
Love, patience, and acceptance
Has already set me free
It is now time
For you to be released
For the duration of my life
The souls that were sacrificed
Cannot be resurrected
In their place
Is scar tissue
Inside the hearts of loved ones
And the deprivation
That has enhanced
My character
I plead for your empathy
I am not worthy of your sympathy
Shatter these chains
That constrict the breath of my family
It is getting late
Please do not keep my mother awake
Waiting
With tears flooding her grave
Allow her tortured specter to rest
Allow me to come home
I have found the path
This pen is my heart
I am bleeding these words out to you

Can you understand?

Gifts of Love...

Marc Ching

Dearest father,
how could I not come to your doorstep
bearing gifts
of love that express the true meaning of my heart,
gifts of promise that connect my every thought
to you
like I was born umbilically.

How could I not come to your doorstep with something
more than I already have
showing signs of progress through successes
I have created on my own.
Intellect, creativity, ingenuity
gathered up like sticks as I walked through the forest
kindling, for the one sole purpose
of progress.

How could I not come to your doorstep
with signed petitions of my respect
illustrating the footprints I have left across the sands
and on people's hearts.
Blueprints of complexities narrowed down to simplistic
solutions
symbolic of these Hollywood search lights
illuminating my purpose and place
in the desperate search

for who I am.
Wanting to be something
I could never understand until now
pushing, pressing, pinning, fighting
just to be like you,
humble in your own quiet dwelling
where thieves would love to learn
your secrets, I watched
and through your eyes all I see
is my reflection.

Dearest mother,
how could I not come to your doorstep
bearing gifts
of love that express the true meaning of my heart,
gifts of promise that connect my every thought
to you
like I was born umbilically.

How could I not come to your doorstep
holding a thousand roses
each one containing the true essence of my purpose
blossoming with memories of glorious moments
we've shared throughout time,
memories that have shaped the personality of my soul
delivering definition, meaning, life
cutting away and toning.
A mind filled with the many lessons we have learned –
together…
catching one another along the way, carrying
rocking back and forth when I was young
trusting in the only safety I knew, You.

How could I not come to your doorstep
with thank you cards
nine thousand four hundred and seventy,
for each day of my life
signed with black ink in languages foreign to others
and secret to ourselves
thanking you for monumental birthdays,
shoyu chicken and yearbooks.
I know it hasn't been easy, my grip
squeezing every last tear from your body, depriving
draining all life force from you,
your milk so pure with intentions
providing the essential antibodies I need in life
to fight off infection.
Yes, my every existence tilts on a pendulum
balanced by you
and through your iris I see only miracles
that you have done,
cultivated by the touch of your hands
with calloused finger tips
you still,
love me…

When Will I See Her Again?

Eddy Zheng

"Why won't you visit your aunt? Did you forget me?" My aunt inquired for the fourth time. "Your Mom and Dad visited; your brother and sister came back to see me, and they even brought their sons. When are you going to come see me?" She kept asking. I didn't get a chance to respond. "Of course, I didn't forget you. I think of you all the time. I will come see you soon. I love you, GuMa." She didn't want to hear what I had to say. It's not her fault she doesn't believe me. This is the first time I've spoken to her since I left her crying in China on a cold day in November 1982…

We were standing on the platform of the train station in Canton, China. GuMa was there to say farewell to the family. Her eyes were red and swollen from crying for the last few days. She was doing her best to choke back the tears welling in her eyes. She had been with the family my whole life. I held her firm and weathered hand pleading with her not to cry. I promised to write even though she could not read. I promised I would go visit when I was old enough. I didn't understand why she couldn't come to America with the whole family. I left her the ceramic piggy bank with my life's savings to make sure she had some extra money after I was gone. GuMa squeezed my little hands and promised me, "I will be all right." The train gradually pulled out of the station and my face was glued to the window so I could get one last glance of GuMa standing there wiping her eyes.

Among the members of my family, I was the closest with GuMa. Not until I was older did I understand exactly how much GuMa loved me, sacrificing to make sure I was cared for. She raised me while my parents worked and my sister and brother were in school. She tended to all my basic needs. When I got up in the morning, breakfast was waiting for me. She would get the water ready for me, help wash my face, and make sure I brushed my teeth. After school, she would have lunch and dinner ready. My clothes were hand-washed everyday. Whenever we ate my favorite dish, soy sauce chicken, she always gave me the best and biggest piece of meat – the thigh. Of course, she had a special dessert for me too, home-baked egg cake. I loved GuMa's cooking.

Whenever I was in trouble, she would stick up for me and protect me from any harsh punishment. When it was hot during the summer months, she would fan me to sleep at night. When it was cold during the winter months, she would let me stick my little feet between her legs to get

Untitled ✦ *Hyung-Rae* (2005), ink on paper

warm. My cold feet usually made her whoop and holler, but not once did she deny me. There must have been a million things GuMa did for me.

Here I am on the telephone talking to GuMa, who is thousands of miles across the globe, for the first time in fourteen years. I feel that she is right next to me. I expected her to cry when she heard my voice on the telephone. Then she would be overjoyed and tell me how much she missed me, ask me how I'm doing. Instead, all I heard was pain and disappointment in her voice. Though advanced technology enables me to talk to GuMa as if she is sitting before me, it cannot bridge the chasm that turns us into strangers. After all she has done for me, how can I be so cold-blooded and not write to her, call her or visit her? I realize that she is laying a guilt trip on me. She has every right to do so. I have no excuse. I didn't know how I would feel when I finally had a chance to call her. I anticipated an overwhelming emotion that would make me cry. I didn't. The person who was once my protector and best friend rejected me. The bond that GuMa and I once had was no longer there. My expectations were too high. What gives me the right to expect her forgiveness after I abandoned her fourteen years ago? Could I ever tell GuMa that the only reason I didn't go back to China and visit is that I'm in prison!? Would the truth allow me to redeem my callous actions? Would she then understand the pain that I went through not being able to tell her the truth? Would that be enough? I don't know. All I know is that life sucks!

Many times I've expressed to friends that before I die, the two people I would want to see are my Mom and GuMa. For now, the pleading voice of GuMa echoes in my head: "When are you coming to see me?"

"Soon." I say. ✦ ✦ ✦

Difficult Chanting Sutras

Eddy Zheng

"He's too busy with college. The school won't allow him to take a leave," is one of Mom's many ingenious excuses to relatives, explaining why I couldn't make it to Grandpa's funeral. If you say it long enough, you just may believe it. Maybe that's the way Mom deals with the pain of losing her "little precious treasure" - what she has always called me - to prison.

I have been locked up in prison for the past fourteen years. The saddest thing is that, to this date, none of my relatives and my childhood friends know about it. There is an old Chinese saying: "Every family has a book of difficult chanting sutras." No matter how content people's families may appear to be, they all have some dark secrets or struggles that no one knows about. Hiding the fact that I'm incarcerated from friends and relatives is one of our family's difficult chanting sutras.

Like many other families on holidays doubled as family reunions, ours got together to celebrate. Each household was designated to be the host for the holiday of its choice. It is a tradition. On the day of the reunion, all the relatives get together to go to movies, parks, play MahJong, and catch up on current events with other members of the family. When it's dinner time, the adults sit around the table eating and talking about their families. It is an opportunity for all the relatives to brag about how well their children are doing and how financially stable they are. Nobody talks about any difficulties or problems they might be having. If they did, they would be losing face in front of the relatives. This often leads to gossiping outside of the family.

As children, we had our own table next to the adults. We would eat, tease each other, watch television and laugh our heads off. During those gatherings, I got to bond with my grandparents, aunts, uncles, and cousins. Most importantly, having reunions year round made us a close knitted family. It was rare that someone would miss a family reunion.

There is no way I can be away in school for fourteen years without going home for a visit or attending any of the reunions. If that were true, I must have gotten a dozen academic degrees by now. In the beginning of my incarceration, when relatives asked about me, Mom would say, "Eddy is busy studying in school far away. It's inconvenient for him to come home, but he calls me all the time. He comes home for visits when he can. You guys just missed him." On the rare occasions that I call home while my aunt and uncle are visiting, I have to tell them the same lie. It wouldn't be wise to go against Mom's good intention to protect the family shame from spreading. So I tell them that I'm extremely busy with school and working at the same time. They ask me to visit them when I do go home. I say yes. Then I have to cut our phone conversation off because prison rules only allow calls to last fifteen minutes. In the beginning, the relatives might have believed Mom's excuses for my absence. However, after not seeing or talking to me for a few years, I'm sure some of them have speculated that the reason I'm never home is not because I'm in school. They just stop asking about me so they don't have to hear the same excuses Mom has been telling them.

It was unrealistic for my relatives to accept Mom's explanation that I was too busy to go to Grandpa's funeral. Then a year later, when my grandma passed away, I couldn't make it to her funeral either. Surely, Mom didn't expect the relatives to believe that I was too busy with school and couldn't get away, again. Why would Mom go out of her way to lie about the fact that I'm in prison? Did she do it out of love or out of shame? Is she in denial?

I can only imagine how difficult it is for Mom to cover up the fact that I'm in prison serving a life sentence. She has to tell a lie every time someone asks about me. She can't lift her head up in front of the relatives at family reunions, knowing that they're wondering what has happened to me. She has to hide the letters I send home, so no one will see them. She can't display the photographs we take in our visits since the blue prison uniform would uncover her lie. She blames my imprisonment on her poor parenting skills. She has to live with the fact that her youngest son had to grow up in prison instead of by her side. She wants to protect the family's reputation the best way she knows how.

Why would Mom go out of her way to lie about the fact that I'm in prison? Did she do it out of love or out of shame? Is she in denial?

I discussed with Mom the idea of telling the truth concerning my prison confinement to my grandparents while they were alive. They were in their seventies and their health was deteriorating. I wanted to have a chance to hold their weathered hands and tell them how much I loved them. I couldn't write letters to them because they would have known from the return address that I was in prison. I couldn't call them because I was only allowed to make collect calls, which would indicate that the calls came from a prison.

I wanted to have a relationship with Grandma and Grandpa. They were the ones who traveled all the way to China and arranged for my family to come to America so we could have a better future. I never had a chance to bond with them when I was a teenager. By the time I was sentenced to do life with a possibility of parole in prison, it was too late for me to get to know them. I was only sixteen years old. That was when the lie that I was away in school started. They have given my family and me so much love, by enabling us to live in better conditions. Yet to me, they were strangers. I wanted to ask them about our family history. I wanted to know about the sufferings, culture shocks, language barriers, and racism that they experienced while growing up in America during the early 20th century. I wanted to know about the struggles that they endured and overcame as Asian Americans. I wanted to know how they felt when the Chinese Communist Party forbade them to go back to their motherland to visit their children. I wanted to know what their favorite colors were, smell their silver hair, and give them big hugs and kisses only a grandson would know how to give – gently wrapping my arms around their waists and lightly touching their foreheads with my lips. Those are some out of thousands of questions I had - and still have - for Grandpa and Grandma.

I didn't know how I would break the news of my incarceration to them, but I was willing to tell the truth. Mom denied my request after some serious contemplation. She had her logical reasoning: "You know that your grandparents have heart problems. I don't think they can handle the news at this stage. You don't want to be the cause of their death, do you? Right now, they think that you're doing well in college and working. They're happy. We have kept the secret from them for these many years. Let's just keep it that way. At least when they die they can go peacefully by not knowing. It's best for everyone. I know it's hard on you; you just have to accept it." What else could I say? The last thing I wanted to do was to be the cause of my grandparents' death.

For now, our family's book of difficult chanting sutras continues to be my hindrance. It prevents me from having relationships with my relatives and gaining freedom to reveal the truth of my incarceration. Whenever family reunions come around, I can visualize Mom getting ready to recite what has become her instinctive mantra: "Eddy is too busy with college." ✦ ✦ ✦

Untitled ◆ *Hyung-Rae* (2005), ink on paper

Npau suav txog
Los tsis pom ntsej muag
Tsis hnov suab
Zoo li nyob ntawm
Ntsej muag kiag
Cev tes mus
Los tsis chwv
Mus ze npaum cas
Los zoo li
Haj yam deb tas

Ci ntsa iab
Cuag li hnub qub
Tiam sis zoo li
Tsaus tshaj qhov tsua

Ib ntsais muag
Ploj kiag
Sawv dheev
Kua muag nrog heev

Xav kom Niam tes los so
Mam nco
Niam sia twb tso

Tsis paub koj
Zoo li cas
Ces hauv kub siab
Tuav koj npe
Ib hnub
Yeej yuav tau
Tuav koj tes

Rau txog hnub ntawv
Yeej yuav nco koj rawv

Only in Dreams

Ricky Thor
(Luav Thoj)

Dreamt of yet
There's no face
No voice

It's right here
In front of me
When reached for
Can't touch
Move closer yet
Only seem further

Bright
As a star
Yet feels dark
As a cave

One blink
It's gone
Wake up
Tear Drops

Wish the hands of Mom
Would wipe the tears
Then remembered
Her life wasn't spared

Don't know how
You look like
So in my heart
Your name I'll hold tight

To hold your hand
One day I'll get
Missing you
I'll never forget

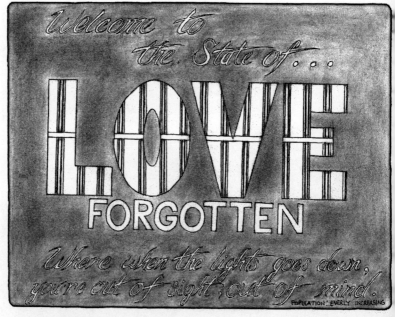

Untitled ◆ *Ricky Thor* (2005), pencil on paper

Waiting

K.D. Huynh

Took a long shower today. Trying to wash all my pain away. Ain't no use, it's like endless water flowing down the drain. In fact, it intensifies the pain. Cause memories gather like fallen rain. Driving me to the point of going insane. And so another day has gone by. I guess time does fly. I'm still thinking about you all the time. You will always be inside my mind. But you're out there and I'm in here. Wet and dried up tears throughout the years. And I wrote this letter in my head. I thought that so many things were left unsaid. Now you're gone and I can't seem to think straight. Funny, how I used to believe in fate.

But…this could be the one last chance to make you understand. To prove somehow all that I can. If there was just one wish I could be granted here tonight. It would be to have you right back by my side to hold tight. For I'd do anything just to hold you in my arms. Everything, to be with you and keep you warm. To try to make you laugh and bring you smiles. To make it up to you and worth your while. Anything and everything to prove that my love is true. And to fall asleep and dream with you.

So now…maybe after all these years. If you even remember or miss me…just know that I'm still waiting here. ✦ ✦ ✦

Have I Ever Told You?

Teng Ntsis Vang

Have I ever told you just how beautiful you look?
If one was to describe your beauty,
It'll be like writing a book.
Your eyes, so lovely and bold they are,
one that seems to twinkle with great captivation,
like that of the celestial stars.
Your smile,
If only one can see will melt even those
with a hardened heart and make the strong
weak in the knees.
Your mere presence is but breathless, and
touching profoundly
one's heart, reaching to the core of one's soul.

Have I ever told you
just how desirous you are?
It's like drinking the sweetest nectar
leaving one longing for more.
You're just that type of person
that one cannot help own strength and determination.
Try to make all your hopes and dreams come true
'cause you are like the moon and the stars
that makes the heavens bright.

For without you
what would be of the beauty that exists
only in the night and what of the day?
For sure you are like the sun
'cause without your warm tender rays
life would exist for no one.
But these are just my thoughts
as I watch the sun rise gently kissing the morning dew,
pondering yet to myself,
wondering…

Have I ever told you?

✦ ✦ ✦

Not Even a Thought

Teng Ntsis Vang

I sit up at night
while my heart burns with passionate flames.

Listening to the soothing wind
as it gently whispers your name.

I'm lost in deep thoughts for my thoughts are of you.

I'm longing for something I can't have.

It's just a wish that I know would not come true
for who would want a man
who lives and yearns for something.

Something that he cannot have.

Npau Suav Txog Koj

Teeb Ntsis Vaj

Tus nkauj Hmoob zoo li lub hnub qub,
muaj tau nkaum ob xyoo no lawm cas kuv
nyob ib leeg tsis muaj koj? Leej twg dhag
rau koj tias kuv tsis hlub koj lawm? Tsis
txhob ntseeg vim kuv tseem hlub koj.

So lub kua muag es txob pub poob lawm,
xav ncav kom cuag koj, tuav kuv phab tes
es cia kuv puag koj ntawm kuv xwb ntiag.
Kuv yeej tsis xav tso koj li, tsis tau hlub ib
tug npaum koj. Thaum wb sib tuav tes sib
tawb ua si luag ntxhi kuv thiab koj zoo siab
tshaj lub ntiaj teb.

Tus nkauj Hmoob kuv hlub, ua npaum li
cas niab hnub niab hmo kuv xam tsis pom
koj. Leej muam los no los cia kuv tuav koj,
cia kuv nwj koj, cia kuv ntxhi rau koj hais
tias kuv hlub koj. Hmo no kuv mas npau
suav kom kuv pom koj, cia wb txoj kev sib
hlub nyob mus tas ib txhis. ✦ ✦ ✦

Girl, Can I Speak for a Minute?

Fernando Sumagit

Chorus:

Girl, can I speak for a minute
to let you know what I'm feeling
our separation isn't making our relationship easy
but if we just hold on living it day to day
patiently wait for me baby and not to throw it away
remembering our love is true and it surpasses it all
our love can grow even though I'm living
inside of the wall
my love for you is on fire and I refuse to give up
that ain't gonna keep me forever we shouldn't make it
that rough

Verse 1:

You know it's up to you and I to see our love survive
that if we really loved each other it'll stand through time
believe in love don't ever let it leave from your sight
I know it gets lonely holding your pillow at night
don't ever cease to reminisce on memories that we shared
whenever you were in trouble how I was always there

and this is just another obstacle to build our bond
to have us stand in the storm but love will take us beyond
everyday from dusk till dawn I'm placing wood on the fire
giving the best that I could do for love to never retire
baby it don't have to be the end if our love is true
I wouldn't ever leave your side if this shit happened to you
so let me know that you love me
and that you'll always be mine
I can't allow us to throw away the years of our lives

Verse 2:

I'm hoping you can forgive me for all the wrong
that I've done
and that I do apologize for leaving you all alone
and that I really try to understand your side of the story
you probably deserve better
I have the right to be worried
but if you wanted to leave before you do let me say
that I appreciate you lady in a million of ways
I probably haven't been the best
and gave you reasons to leave
but baby girl I'm hoping you can try to believe
I know it hasn't been easy for you to deal with the stress
and I'm responsible for even have created this mess
what reasons have I to give for you to stay and be true
I ain't got none all I can say is that I promise to you
that I will be a better man and live the way you desire
so that you know that you love me without a doubt,
there's a fire
one that you know you can trust
one to believe that it's right
whenever you ask the question if it was worth it to fight

Mom's Unconditional Love

Fernando Sumagit

Chorus:

Mom's unconditional love my mama's loving trust

the strength that my mama gave me
helps me to wipe off the dust

hope and compassion believing in me all of the time

told me to make out a demo so they can all hear my rhymes

inside my dreams she's still alive like yesterday

I hear her voice speaking to me within her delicate grace

the memories still live on to be strong and forever

watching over us from the heavens
praying that life gets better

Verse:

Words that would always encourage came from my baby girl

the precious love from a woman open my eyes to the world

who gave me love the courage to be strong and be wise

the one who said I was able to spread my wings and to fly

follow my heart and my dreams that if I fall to get up

and if I want it go get it don't ever cease or give up

to climb as high as I want right there in case I do fall

always had something to teach me and had a story to tell

and if I failed she would say that I'll know better next time

I thank the man up in heaven
that the dear woman was mine

pure and divine forever in my heart and my mind

to reach my goals of succession
to seek and search and to find

if asked to define my mama no words could describe

love and devotion was given and so instilled inside

someone to always believe in even when times were rough

especially when the weather was beating down so tough

giving me hope to move on breathing upon me a kiss

writing me so many letters to let me know that I'm missed

guiding me through it taking me step by step how to do it

and when I finally did it you tell me how much you knew it

tears falling on me from heaven which lets me know
that you're there

all of the time you invested professes how much you care

walking along your shadow living the dreams you inspire

the intuition you gave the hopes you always desired

inside my heart you're the fire gives me the courage to strive

the demonstration of faith for willingness just to try

you gave me love
that surpasses the mountaintops of the Alps

the hours you spent on teaching me all the ins and the outs

I love you mama forever be the light of my life

the woman knew what she's doing
giving me the will to survive

❖ ❖ ❖

Perspectives

Untitled

Dạt Nguyen

Lately, all I seen are wicked demons,
the baddest of the bunch,
result of the meanest semen,
gangstas and riders, pros in their professions,
tattoos and battle scars are their only confession,
gun towers, barbed wire fences, and brick walls,
if you are falling, then pick yourself up and stand tall,
living with lions and vultures
coming off lockdown
all tattooed up is just prison's culture,
slammed down, read books just to pass the time
lockdown and still working towards my prime
if I plant a seed now, will it grow?
and if my dream grows big, will it soar?
will they water it? or will they simply destroy it?
at sixteen, my dream shattered,
when they told me it was all good, I was flattered!
since fourteen, I started seeing demons crawl,
they creeped and they crawled on the walls of the hall
smiling at me as I scraped my set on the door
following me wherever I go,
got the judge upset, attached to strings like a puppet,
as soon as I step in the room, my future was set,
by my tight eyes, I was judged by people I've never met.

Untitled ◆ *Dat Nguyen* (2005), ink on cloth

To Whom It May Concern

Đạt Nguyen

To whom it may concern:
to whoever that can relax
and watch the youth's futures burn,
it's about our youth and their consequences,
sixteen-year-old youngsters
get sent inside of these prison fences
and told that they'll get out one day,
let's do a month in this yard
and let's see what you have to say,
rehabilitation, yet it is full of shhh,
a gang of riders waiting for you to get with
if they do a full-term without a mission,
then they never did a term inside of hell's kitchen:
level 4, 180-yard,
lockdown every other month,
let's see who can travel far,
270 and level 3 is safe
and if you mess up, it's gurney not a wheelchair,
the one involved straight to the hole,
mandatory SHU term even if it's not a goal,
if you know something, just sit back and watch the show,
and if you are a mark, you'll be the last one to know.

Shhh pops off the guard screams, "down!"
don't sit right away; just look around,
ain't nothing nice getting caught in a crossfire,
block guns and mini-14's rang-out with the guard's desire,

when nothing is up they'll lock you down,
make up bullshhh like weapons been found,
wait 'til two months and they'll do a shakedown,
never find knives, just want to toss your house,
lockdown comes and goes, sometimes it'll be for a while,
better be prepared with those canteen goods
because you'll get sick off of this state food,
coming off the lockdown all tattooed up,
head to toes no more space, tat up a few cups,
after a year, you're going to see committee,
screw with your points, make sure no level 3,
points keep adding on, make sure you'll never leave,
grab a cup of pruno to put yourself at ease.,
shots of white lightning will be ready to pour,
down it quick and make sure you can handle yours,
drink to the end and cough up blood,
living the life years after years,
tears run dry and heart turns cold,
only the fortunate one will hit parole,
with 70% of the population lifers,
day by day walk the yard as riders.

Let's say you hit parole one day,
with two strikes with a whole different game to play,
after a decade and a half, locked away
and let's say you stroll the right way,
enjoy life free, living day by day,
maybe your lil' cousin, nephew,
or the lil' homie from the set,
eyes wide shut idolizes the big homie he just met,
never heard a word from the game that you left him,
all he knows is the 5-0 and his enemies out to get him,
checking out your tattoos and admiring the life,
can't wait until he gets there, he's going to get his stripes,
can't you see homie you're just in jail?
and if you keep screwing up, you'll be sent to hell,
your future will not be in our hands, but someone else's
doing hard time, blaming nobody but yourself,
so just do your time and do it for yourself
or you'll mess up your life and the next generation as well,
think about your lil' brother or cousin riding their bicycle,
do the right thing, keep yourself and them out of the cycle.

Untitled ◆ *Hyung-Rae*, (2004) ink on paper

Ghost

Eddy Zheng

If you go out at night
you will see a ghost one day.

The warning and wisdom of a mother
a prophecy unheeded.

I lay under the covers of a fluffy bed
fully dressed awaiting for the sleepy bugs
to close my parents' tiring eyes.

It's almost midnight
I tiptoe to the rhythm
of my parents' breathing like a burglar
and enter the bathroom.

As I open the window
I flush the toilet to disguise the sound and crawl out
standing on the ledge of the second floor apartment building
I wonder how I will get down to the ground.

Fear is not in the vocabulary
of an invincible 15-year-old.

I slide down the black drainage pipe
only to face a 10-foot fence blocking my way.

The alluring darkness hypnotizes me
turning back is not an option
I climb over the fence and disappear
in darkness.

As I lay under the covers of a stiff double bunk bed
on this modern-day slave plantation called the Prison
Industrial Complex
the ghost sleeps with me.

◆ ◆ ◆

the Real Me

Viêt Mike Ngo

In a dimly lit classroom, I sit alone at an oaken table. I sit and envy the wood underneath my fingers. I wonder if its silent exterior belie what's underneath. Is it like what's inside of me? A sea of fire and acid, anger and frustration. Is there a wounded spirit who wants to escape into the tangible world and destroy its substance, hating its makers? I want my insides to be like the oaken table - real. Instead there's only an emptiness; an emptiness that wants more than it's name whispered in the wind; wanting more than it's shadow splayed across a sidewalk; not getting either. Can skin contain this craving for retribution? this churning of emotions into steel; sharp and ungiving; this weapon forged from hatred and cooled in frustration?

A sliver of sunlight slips underneath a door and is absorbed by the cinder-block walls painted brown. I want my spine to have this osmosis quality so that I may have warmth instead of fire or ice. Sunlight, spread along my limbs and cleanse the raw wound left in the soil of my being. Dissolve the jagged edged rocks protruding from my chest. Fill me with growth that is never-ending. Change me from within so that what emerges from this cocoon is not a sword or wasp or monster, but a butterfly: A fragile baby testing its wings for a current of air. Let me have a life unscarred by war.

I sit alone in a crowded room and my heart beats butterfly wings to a rhythm only I and "God?" can hear. One head in a sea of black hair. One floating seaweed adrift in a sea of black hair. How did I wind up on this deserted island? I sit alone and wonder if a butterfly can make it back home across this sea of black hair.

So I write. I write to say what I know and to find out what I don't. I write for love, the love of the young and old; for the energy that is me. I want people to love me and writing is my funnel to their mouths. I write for history. I write for my ancestors whose history is lost in a grave site; whose stories are only heard by worms. I write for the future: for the next generation so they'll know who I was. The I who lived and killed and died. I write so my nephew will know me in a way I don't know my uncles; the dead from war, the ones dead from life. I want to carry him on my words, teach him to fly with verbs, soothe him with nouns; sounds from my mind, through my pen, to his heart. I want him to know the real me.

And I write for me; for the visions calling me when I lay on my bunk and look at pictures of a past life. These visions are voices, these voices are words forgotten by man, except from me. I carry their burden. I am their savior - my nephew, my ancestors, their worms. ✦ ✦ ✦

Red, White and Blue

Việt Mike Ngo

A group of men sit inside a room inside a prison. In this room maps of the world adorn the walls. These men are writing and talking about a war. This is our war room and we are the vanguards of the Revolution. There are no soldiers or generals, yet all are soldiers and generals.

What is this war about? It is about all that is golden.

Who are we fighting? We are fighting all that is red, white and blue.

They call us murderers and psychopaths. They are the same ones who muddied their boots on land where my ancestors roamed. They are the same ones with camouflaged helmets who forced my ancestors into oblivion. And they call us murderers. My ancestors whose necks lie under those muddy boots.

Where are you now, my Ancestors? Do you call me? Do you call us? I see the world wrapped around the room wrapped around my mind and I wonder are there other men and women who are waging war against them; these "them" that I remember being taxied home in tin boxes wrapped in red, white and blue.

Red, white and blue: Where did these colors come from? Red is the blood on their hands as they strangle the weak. White are the eyes and teeth of their victims. Blue is our future set in motion for "them." ✦ ✦ ✦

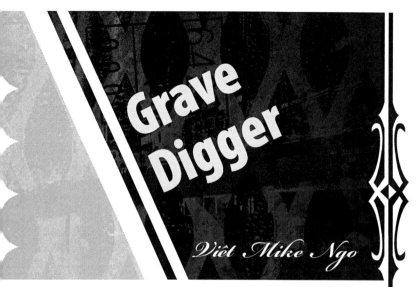

Grave Digger

Việt Mike Ngo

We all have roles to play. Some are grave diggers, others fill them. Some decide what shovels to use, others decide who goes where. We all have roles to play and it saddens me to know my role has nothing to do with what I like or what I want.

I don't want war. I want a hammock and a guitar, a beach and some shade. I want to feel the ocean lapping at my ankles and see children smiling. I want the sweetness of coconut milk and the spiciness of a kiss under the waves. I want love and peace.

But dreams don't live in graveyards. Fillers of graves don't have that luxury. My role is to dig or be dug out. Some may say this kind of change is unproductive. I say these "some" don't live in grave yards. Or if they do, they forgot the smell of wholeness; they forgot because the stink has commensurated with the marrow of their souls, and now this smell seems natural; and they forgot that to purge this stink, we need graves and diggers.

So while some preach reform inside classrooms and churches, I'll sharpen my shovel. For revolutions need graves. Revolutions need diggers to fill them. You fill the desks and pews. I'll fill the graves. We all have roles to play. ✦ ✦ ✦

it does not have to be this way!

Untitled ◆ *Bucky Thor* (2005), pencil on paper

All Around Me

Ricky Thor

All around me I feel sorrow

All around me I sense pain

I hear laughter

I see joy

But they only fool themselves

With their pride

Religious they claim to be

Sheep a wolf can seem

Saint I am not

Committed this crime I did not

Punishment from the start I got

I was still a tot

In a hell I am in

Locked up in this pen

Forgiveness He claims to give

This life I still have to live

Memories of my Mother I have none

Disowned by brother I have done

Shame on my Father I have brought

Out of mind from my Family

I have not sought

Love I try to find

From this cage of mine

A time they will spare

To stay

They will fade

Living in this Hell

Saint Anger dwell

Till redemption day

I will keep it away

A Place Called Poetry

Marc Ching

Absent in my palms
I throw out my hands to you.

Stretching for freedom
everyday I lose another word
another breath that whispered
"how can my world tell you who I am"
your fingerprints
could remove the scars that shackle me
to a place where angry men spend all their time waiting.

How can I find my way to you
in the darkness
I disguise myself in your poetry
each broken piece painted with your words
the ink of your pen connecting us together.

When we meet
your pale feel press softly on the edge of my paper
sometimes when I see you
your world scratched onto paper
you bring me in pieces
stories that help me take back
return to me a part of what they took

everyday it is always
everyday I save your page
hold the bookmark up against my heart
I will wait for you there.

And at night
I make love to the cool breeze
the winter rain cleanses me of sin
have too many years passed between us
has the water washed away all that we have worked to
create,
I loved you the only way I knew
always an impossible task
our hands stretching out to find freedom

and still
there are times
when I breathe in the colors that push from your pen
when I paint my world in that same bouquet of syllables
in those same whispers that never leave me until
the blue sky bleeds into the night
until
the darkness pushes me back into my palms
back into this place we call poetry
where words have made us into gods
where our pain has set us free from suffering.

Because there have been nights like this one
nights in which
if we don't fight they will kill us anyways
take back their last signs of weakness
take back that piece of heaven you have given me.
I've learned to face death in a way by watching you
your silent hands that know what they love
if they touch me
the darkness could never take me away
would you lead me out into the wildness.

I know in a way
but it has been five and a half years now
there is nothing that my time can repay
everyday they destroy something that was good
my hands write nothing that my blood would not bleed
or die for

in the face of necessary struggle
no ink will be shed in words that I myself have not spoken.

I know their arms must ache without me
you once told me
"life is only as big as what we make of it"
my world cannot exist without you
just as the moon cannot orbit around the stars,
you told me if I stretched out to find God
that He would erase all the darkness from within me
but five and a half years have passed since then
and the blue sky still bleeds into the night
pushing me back into this place we call poetry
where words have made us into gods
where our pain has set us free from suffering
but it has not made me regret
only question
how long must one person suffer for an action.

I still believe though
in that same hour you will come to me
in hands that know what they love
in hands that can remove the scars that shackle me
liberate us with the purity of words
my iris looks at the world through fragile pupils
we are not strong as we may seem
lost in a place called poetry.

But it is never the same
the last words I remember you hearing
nor is the dream when you first showed me the stars,
you were right when you told me
love will not be enough on this journey
if only you had asked me then
I would have returned to you without resistance
crucified my words on the cross for your salvation
when will you lead me out into wildness
my hands absent without you
still stretching to find freedom.

124

Cut No Corners or Half Step

Fernando Sumagit

Chorus:

I can't allow myself to cut no corners or half step
to handle all of my business till I don't have none left
keeping my head above water building my brain to be smart
staying ahead of my game keeping my aim toward the stars
constantly moving I'm at it to keep myself well prepared
cuz wen it's time to get funky I know how to take it there
professional dedication pure and devoted to rock
ain't nothing easy that's why I kept it hard not to stop

Verse 1:

It's been a long road for me and I don't came too far
growing up all alone and on my own raised in bars
only able to look up at the stars locked up in walls
they wanna talk to me they'd write a letter no one can call
I fell too much it hurt so much but learned to get back up
and every time I got better at dealing with such
containing pain in my body seeking to rise to the top
sometimes I don't feel like pushing but then not able to stop
gotten addicted to be determined to fight
and even if the sun was up or down day or night
inside of me I've developed endurance building my strength

creative plus innovative is how I deal with my pain
using my wit take a chance taking a risk when I dance
I can't be cutting no corners cuz that ain't how I enhance

Verse 2:

I'm Filipino and young G out of North San Jose
all of my life as I recall locked in a cage
serving my time all alone so far as out to Nevada
with playas from Colorado even South Bend Indiana
growing up hard and frying in the summer sun
don't wanna give up my life so I'm a stick to my guns
putting it down live committed to be determined to stride
don't be no half step for that ain't gonna be the way to survive
do what the weak minded don't don't let'em pass me "I won't"
turning my weakness into motivation "What you ain't know?"
smile in my face but I'm smashing leaving 'em way back behind
they all gonna do what they do me constantly seek to find
I spent my years living blinded falling upon to the ground
not getting nowhere I searched and now look what I've found
a desperation to make it an opportunity taken
game that was given I used it for the dream I've been chasing.

✦ ✦ ✦

Interview with "Peaches"

Eddy Zheng
with Peaches

I want you to make a mental picture of the Chinese movie star Zhang Ziyi. Now picture Zhang Ziyi in an all-male prison. Can you imagine what life would be like? Peaches, a Vietnamese American homosexual, knows what it is to live like this.

I met Peaches in San Quentin State Prison around 2001. Peter is his/her birth name. He/she identifies as an Asian Queen. Being a Queen always sticks out like a sore thumb in prison, especially an Asian Queen because there aren't that many in the system. Whether it's out of curiousity or lust, some guys are always fighting for the Queen's attention. For many prisoners, being with a Queen is the closest they'll get to being with a woman. Peaches did a short term and was paroled. It wasn't until I saw Peaches in Solano State Prison for a parole violation in 2004 that I'd decided to do this interview.

Eddy: Please tell me something about yourself and family.

Peaches: My birth name is Peter, but I'm known as Peaches. I was born in San Jose, CA. I have a mom, stepfather, and half-brother. My Dad was half French and half Vietnamese. He passed away before I was born. I'm a quarter French mixed with Vietnamese. I'm 25 years old.

E: How do you identify yourself?

P: I'm a woman, but I'm my own species of woman. There is only me, not a category based on society. There's only one me, no one can live my lifestyle. The only time I consider myself as a male is when I'm in prison. When I'm on the street, my driver's license states I'm female. They look at me as who I am and bypass any doubts.

E: Why do you consider yourself a woman?

P: My personality and my choice of lifestyle.

E: Have you ever considered having a sex change?

P: Yes, eventually I'll have it. Right now I need to have a family. When I have everything, then I'll make a change. I don't want to be a Mom and my son say my Mom has a wee-wee. I'll adopt children.

E: When did you realize that you're different?

P: I found out I was different as long as I can remember, around 4 to 6 years old. I knew because I had a crush on a little boy. I didn't get involved with someone until I was 17. I met someone and had feelings for him. He became a big part of my life. He showed me a lot about life. I didn't know what a relationship was until it happened.

E: Have you been abused as a child?

P: Yes, I have been mentally, physically, and emotionally abused as a child.

E: What was it like growing up being different?

P: I was blessed with good friends. I lived a normal life. People are more receptive of me. I dated men. I lived 24/7 as Peaches. My friends were very supportive. The older I got, the easier it was. My family found out I was different when I was 17. My mother accepted me more when I was 22. I was so normal that they accepted me. They don't know that I've been in prison. I have no restriction for being who I am. I haven't lived with my family since I was 13. I've been living with my friends. I came from a very straight Asian family with high expectations. I knew if I wanted to be who I am I couldn't live under their expectations. They kicked me out of the house because I wasn't doing what they expected. I went to school on and off. I started doing drugs. Partying, hanging out. Meeting a lot of people.

E: Why are you in prison?

P: I started coming to prison at the age of 22. I got off track and started doing drugs. I wasn't happy with myself. I got into check fraud. I was good at it until I finally got caught. This time, a violation, a term of 5 ½ months. I violated my parole by physically getting into a fight with my ex-boyfriend. I let my emotions get the best of my common sense and judgment. I'm here a second time and maybe it took a second time for me to realize that I still need change. Change is good. For me these days, even though I am inside these walls, I continue to change, grow, and learn to make the right choices…I've learned life is a constant struggle, but it's my choice how I choose to live it.

E: How did you feel the first time you were in prison?

P: I was numb. I was tired of what I was doing. Everything happened so quick. I was shocked. I couldn't believe that I was in prison. For the first time I felt very tiny in this great big world.

I heard that they were going to cut my hair short, that I would get raped or pimped. Before I went to prison I saw how others were being treated badly. There's so few Asian queens. I was disrespected, got harassed, and sex talked. I was numb.

E: Did you ever fear for your safety or afraid that someone might rape you?

P: I didn't. I could defend myself. If not, I had other choices. When I was in County jail, people told me I could P.C. up (Protected Custody).

The guards were worried about my safety. A Lieutenant said I looked like I was 16. I was so young. They looked at me as a little girl. I was 22.

E: What is your strategy to survive in prison?

P: My strategy to survive in prison is "acceptance." Acceptance that I am here and that there are rules and regulations made before I came here; these standards made by inmates and the people that run these facilities. I follow them to a certain extent. Being who I am, I must run my own program, keep to myself and do not make any rash decisions or mistakes.

I hung out with all the Vietnamese. I worked and was paid 35 cents an hour. That made me feel grateful that I had so much outside. I wrote letters and called my friend once. Everything was so temporary.

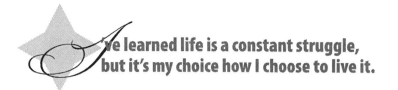

e learned life is a constant struggle, but it's my choice how I choose to live it.

I can't say I had a bad time. I was well taken care of. Someone's always there to watch out for me. At times I felt obligated. I felt like for my company I was obligated to go to the yard, to be there.

I talked to a lot of men. They don't have any female companions. I saw other men's pain. That impacted me the most. It came to a point where everyone needed my attention. I had to pick someone or else it would've been turbulent. So I was casually dating this guy. On the street I never had a relationship without sex. In here, I had a choice to say no. No one put pressure on me. People respected me because the way I carried myself.

E: Do you get propositions from other prisoners?

P: Yes, propositions from other prisoners is common. Prison is its own little world. Being who I am, choosing to live the life of a woman in a man's world and so few are like me and the attraction that I cast: a woman, female attraction that men find intriguing, and once they are intrigued, propositions of all kinds are made.

E: What is your philosophy in dealing with relationships?

P: A relationship in prison is very tough, because the main reason is there are so very few like me and being Asian, it is a rarity. My philosophy is to stick to one, and realize that being in a place like prison, feelings are easily overwhelmed and to always remember to look at it at that advantage, and stay strong.

I met someone. He's a great guy. I couldn't help it. I wasn't making promises. I'm more reality-based when it comes to relationships with men. Everything is so temporary in here. The feelings could be lasting. I live by feelings. After I'm gone, we live different lives. I know I'm enjoying this person's company.

E: What was the most difficult thing you had to deal with?

P: It's knowing how much I didn't have control over my life. I couldn't eat what I wanted or go anywhere. I had no control about outside. Knowing I had a life out there, but I couldn't control it.

I learned that prison and the men that reside here are not all bad. They are just like me. People that have made mistakes or had made wrong choices. I realize many are trying to change and rehabilitate like me. I found many kindred spirits on my journey. I'm not saying prison is all nice and dandy. Life in the regular world there are bad people, too, but majority are just trying to prove for a second chance to live life, and they, like myself, are making the choice to change.

Interview with Ou Chiew Saeturn

Eddy Zheng
with Ou Chiew Saeturn

Ou Chiew Saetern was 26 years old at the time of this interview. He is Mien, immigrating to the U.S. with his family from Southeast Asia at a young age. I met him in Solano State Prison in 2003. Ou's nickname was "Short Dog." He was short and he looked younger than his age. He sagged his pants. Short Dog could draw. That was his hustle in prison. He drew the drawing "Asian Prisoners Revolution" featured in this anthology.

I interviewed him as he was getting ready to go home. He gave me a letter (p. 140), written by his nine year old sister. It was touching.

Eddy: How old are you?
Ou: I'm 26 years old.

E: How long have you been locked up?
O: For over nine years. I started when I was in CYA (California Youth Authority) in Preston (Youth Authority in Ione, California). I was 17 years old. I was transferred from YA to DVI (Deuel Vocational Institution, California Department of Correction's reception center) because I got into a couple of fights

with rival gang members. I still had a gang banging mentality. If I'd stayed out of trouble, I would've stayed in YA until I'm 25.

E: What are you in prison for?

O: Gang related shooting. Me and my boys came out of a club, this girl I used to know, one of her friends brought her over. I realized it was a rival gang member. One thing led to another and we started shooting. We had the upper hand because we got access to the gun fast.

E: Why did you want to shoot him?

O: I'm asking the same question myself. I guess I found it necessary at the time. If I don't shoot him, they'll shoot me. I shoot seven times. The guy was paralyzed, couldn't walk no more. He's 18 years old, a gang member too. I asked them whether they bang, he walked up and said what's up blood. I could see the look in his eyes he was scared. He didn't mean to say what's up blood.

E: What gang were you in?

O: The Asian Boyz. It's a Crip gang.

E: How long was your sentence?

O: They gave me 13 years with 85%.

E: How did you feel when you knew that you'll be going away for a long time?

O: I was too young to realize at that time what that meant. I didn't know how long I was going to do. I thought I was going to do a couple of years only.

E: Did you speak English?

O: A little bit, limited. I went to school from 4th grade to 7th grade, then I quit. Why? I wanted to get the things my friends got, things my family couldn't provide for me. I gang bang, hustle on drugs for clothes. I got a big family. Most of my clothes were hand-me-downs. My friends got new clothes. They picked on me. I started cutting classes, grades dropped. They sent me to continuation school for a year to pick up my grades and go back to Junior High, but I never did it. Kick it on the streets.

guess I found it necessary at the time. If I don't shoot him, they'll shoot me. I shoot seven times. I could see the look in his eyes he was scared.

E: **What about your parents? How did they feel about it?**

O: Dad was mad. He said if I don't go to school, don't come home no more. I went to my homeboy's house and hang out on the streets. I didn't go home no more, only once every two months. Since then my Dad don't talk to me no more. To this day, he still doesn't say nothing to me.

E: **How do you feel when your Dad doesn't say anything to you anymore?**

O: As for that, he did me a favor. I don't have to hear from him yell at me anymore. As time went on, I don't know he care anymore. Now, he did his best to keep me out of trouble. He may felt he'd fail, but he didn't. Now I want a relationship with him. Whatever happened in the past is over.

E: **Why do you want a relationship with him?**

O: So I can let him know he didn't fail. I chose to live that life. Now I'm older. I get wiser. Hopefully I can prove to him that I'm a better man and move forward. I want to be there for him when he needs me. He's getting old.

E: **Do you think your Dad loves you?**

O: Back then, no. But now I think so. Back then, I asked him for money, but he didn't give it to me so I thought he didn't love me. Now I know it's not that he doesn't want to give it to me, it's he doesn't have the money.

E: **Who supports you while you're in prison?**

O: I couldn't think of anybody except Mom. I don't ask her for anything because I know she has to take care of my little sister and brother. I want to make sure they have what I didn't have.

E: How do you survive?

O: Draw cards, tattoo. I don't get a lot but I can get by. I hustle. I learned how to draw in jail. I need shampoo and soap. I don't want to ask people. I be myself. Keep my nose out of other people's business, by listening to the older ones, learn from them, how to carry myself. When I first came, a lot of older brothers taught me the things I needed to survive.

E: Who do you miss?

O: My family, especially my Mom and Dad. They're getting old. I don't know what, how long they have. I want to be there for them.

E: What do you miss?

O: Freedom to do whatever.

E: What would you like to do?

O: Go fishing, camping, be with my family. It's been a long time, but I want to go to a Broadway play. I don't care what people think, square-ass goes to plays. Homeboys, I kick it with them, but they weren't there for me, not even a letter to say fuck you. I spent all my teenager life for being down with them boys. I want to work, be with family.

E: How many tattoos do you have? What are they? Why do you have them?

O: I got a lot. I got like the whole right arm filled up. It got violent pictures on it and troublesome. It symbolizes my past life on the outside. I got three Mongolian nomad warriors on my back symbolize my ancestors. I got Mien pride on my chest, it represents my people. I got two guns up there guarding my pride. I also got some gang graffiti.

E: Why did you decide to get them?

O: I guess at the time it looked cool. As time go by I see it as how I look at life. Life is like a piece of paper. I can draw anything on the paper to represent myself. You put in hard work on something things will come out good. It's like life. If you work hard, you'll succeed in the long run. If you get it fast, it doesn't last. No payoff. I guess I lived a fast life.

Homeboys, I kick it with them, but they weren't there for me, not even a letter to say fuck you. I spent all my teenager life for being down with them boys.

E: **How do you think the tattoos are going to affect you on the outside?**

O: I think it's going to affect me a lot. People look at me as a gang banger, negative affect on me.

E: **What do you think would've helped you from going to prison?**

O: If my family was able to give me what I wanted so I won't be laughed at. That would've helped.

E: **What's the biggest lesson you've learned being in prison for nine years?**

O: That your family is the most important thing in the world. Because me and Mom has a good relationship. She's always been there for me. At the time I didn't know what I put her through. Now I know I put her through a lot of pain.

E: **What is the hardest thing you have experienced in prison?**

O: I guess, I don't know. I think it's waking up not knowing what's going to happen to me. Maybe someone has a bad day and want to take it out on me and become a victim. I seen it happened before. Cellie woke up and beat the shit out of him.

E: **Do you regret what you did to the victim?**

O: I don't think I have regret for my victim. I have remorse for his family because he can't walk anymore. They have to take care of him. As for him, if I don't shoot him, he would've shot me.

E: **Who are you?**

O: I see myself as very respectful, polite, a guy who knows he made a lot of mistake and tried to change them.

E: **Do you think the community should fear you?**

O: No, they should have no reason to be, because I'm not the same guy I was nine years ago.

E: **How do you make sure that you won't come back to prison?**

O: First thing, I have to remember prison. Now I have to take care of myself. I'll go to work, be patient. Hopefully I'll get support from family. I can't get sidetracked by all the negative stuff. No fast money. If I keep my mind to it, anything is possible if I work hard.

E: **What are you going to do after you get out?**

O: I have some experience in carpentry. I'll try to open my business so I can sell my artwork. I have a lot of plans and goals, but I can't reach them because I have to finish parole. Hopefully I can get into a Boys and Girls club to talk to teenagers, offer my experience and guide them to be better individuals. I want to help them.

E: **What would you say to them?**

O: My message to them is I know Asian people don't have a lot, just be patient. Go to school, it'll pay off in the long run. You'll get all that. All the gang banging will get you nowhere but jail. Once you're in jail, nobody cares about you. Never forget where your family come from. They work hard to put food on the table and they came to U.S.A. to get us a better chance.

My grandfather always tell me this, "Every boy will become a man one day, but the real man is determined by how he gets up when he falls." What that means to me is every man gonna make some kind of mistakes in his life. A real man is someone who could live up to his mistake and better himself from it.

Endnotes

Saetern was expected to go home on his release date. However, the day before he was to go home, Homeland Security put an immigration hold on him. Instead of going home, Homeland Security agents picked him up from prison and detained him in its facility.

February 19, 2003

Dear Ou,

    Dearest brother be very good you are
so bad that mom and dad are not very
happy about you when are you coming out
I love you be good ok brother I did
see you before send me a picture of you
On your big sister Shied chiew has two baby
name cynthia and julie the oldest is cynthia she
is six year old and julie is three year old be
good so you could come out mom and love
you so much be good so you could come out
and see mom and dad and us I am a
year old be good not long you are going jail
do not fight other people so you could come
out I just hope you don't do anything bad
again like last time you did do very very good
so you could come out and see us I love you.

    Write back as soon as possible.
                        Your sister,
                        Mina Gaetan

140

February 19, 2003

Dear Ou,

Dearest brother, be very good. You are so bad that mom and dad are not very happy about you. When are you coming out? I love you. Be good, ok, brother. I did see you before. Send me a picture of you. Ou, your big sister has two baby. The oldest is six years old youngest is three year old. Be good so you could come out. Mom love you so much. Be good so you could come out and see mom and dad and us. I am nine years old. Be good. Not long you are going jail. Do not fight other people so you could come out. I just hope you don't do anything bad again like last time you did. Do very very good so you could come out and see us.
I love you.

Write back as soon as possible.

Your Sister

Outro

Co-Editor's Note ◆ ◆ ◆

Ben Wang

As the first ever anthology of Asian & Pacific Islander (API) prisoners' writings and artwork, "Other" provides readers with a glimpse of prison from an API perspective. Eddy Zheng, the visionary and initiator of this project, was largely responsible for contacting and recruiting the many contributors for this project. Publishing an anthology of writings from dozens of contributors is no easy feat - try doing it all from behind bars, as Eddy did. Despite being locked up, his ability to connect with people on a very profound level, both inside and outside of the prison system, continues to amaze me. Many of the other contributors in this book also took it upon themselves to contact and recruit their peers to add to this anthology. Members of the Asian Prisoner Support Committee (APSC), who have worked on prisoner support and anti-deportation projects, also recruited contributors for this project. Desis Rising Up and Moving (DRUM) submitted testimonies that they had collected from South Asian detainees who were being held unjustly in immigration detention jails, as well. Despite our best attempts, this first edition of the anthology does lack full representation from everyone in our community (such as only one submission from a female prisoner and one from a transgender prisoner), which goes to show how many more people inside the prison system are still without a voice.

As co-editor, I edited some of the contributors' writings

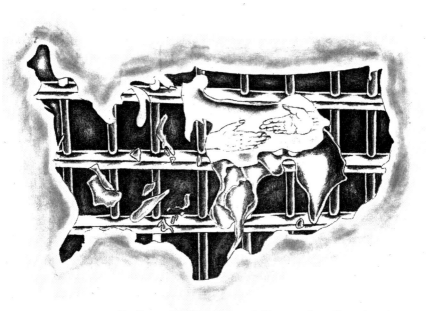

Asian Prisoners Revolution 2 ✦

Ou Chiew Saeturn, pencil on paper

for grammar, spelling, and some structural changes, while striving to keep the author's original meaning intact. When possible, I corresponded with the prisoner contributors to go over my suggested edits and work with them on revising multiple drafts. However, correspondence was not always an option; and even for those to whom I could write letters, editing multiple drafts of work was made arduous by the inconsistent and slow mail system of some prisons.

As this anthology is being sent to the printers, Eddy Zheng remains confined in a northern California immigration detention jail, where he has spent nearly two years fighting his deportation. Unfortunately, many more API community members appear headed towards a similar fate: decades of prison incarceration, topped off with immigration detention and imminent deportation. In response to the U.S.'s addiction to prisons and its status as the world's largest jailer, APSC was re-formed in 2005. APSC works with API prisoners to educate the broader community about the growing number of APIs in the U.S. being imprisoned, detained, and deported. Our mission is to expose the root causes of why more and more APIs are going to prison, such as the crisis of our educational system, the lack of access to resources for low-income immigrants, war, and imperialism.

For those interested in helping to raise awareness about the Prison Industrial Complex and supporting prisoners striving to better themselves and their community, please contact APSC at the address below. We encourage people to correspond with the prisoners, as well. If you would like to write to one of the contributors of this anthology, please send us a letter and we will forward it to them!

Asian Prisoner Support Committee (APSC)
P.O. Box 1031, Oakland, CA 94604
email: apscinfo@gmail.com

More Resources:

Marc Teruo Ching's website for the Prisoner's Reform Organizational Partnership ✦ *www.prisonersreform.org*

Updates and information regarding Eddy Zheng's battle against deportation ✦ *www.eddyzheng.com*

Eddy Zheng's daily online blog ✦ *eddyzheng.blogspot.com*